PRESENTED TO:

_____

FROM:

_____

DATE:

_____

AWAKE AND ALIVE

AWAKE AND ALIVE

A 30-DAY CHALLENGE TO REVIVE YOUR FAITH

MATT CHANDLER

THOMAS NELSON
Since 1798

Awake and Alive

© 2025 by Matt Chandler

All rights reserved. No portion of this book may be reproduced, stored in a retrieval system, or transmitted in any form or by any means—electronic, mechanical, photocopy, recording, scanning, or other—except for brief quotations in critical reviews or articles, without the prior written permission of the publisher.

Published in Nashville, Tennessee, by Thomas Nelson. Thomas Nelson is a registered trademark of HarperCollins Christian Publishing, Inc.

Published in association with Yates & Yates, www.yates2.com.

Thomas Nelson titles may be purchased in bulk for educational, business, fund-raising, or sales promotional use. For information, please email SpecialMarkets@ThomasNelson.com.

Unless otherwise noted, Scripture quotations are taken from the ESV ® Bible (The Holy Bible, English Standard Version®). Copyright © 2001 by Crossway, a publishing ministry of Good News Publishers. All rights reserved.

Scripture quotations marked CEB are taken from the Common English Bible. Copyright © 2011 Common English Bible.

Scripture quotations marked MSG are taken from *The Message*. Copyright © 1993, 2002, 2018 by Eugene H. Peterson. Used by permission of NavPress. All rights reserved. Represented by Tyndale House Publishers, Inc.

Scripture quotations marked NIV are taken from the Holy Bible, New International Version®, NIV®. Copyright © 1973, 1978, 1984, 2011 by Biblica, Inc.® Used by permission of Zondervan. All rights reserved worldwide. www.zondervan.com. The "NIV" and "New International Version" are trademarks registered in the United States Patent and Trademark Office by Biblica, Inc.®

Italics added to direct Scripture quotations are the author's emphasis.

Any internet addresses, phone numbers, or company or product information printed in this book are offered as a resource and are not intended in any way to be or to imply an endorsement by Thomas Nelson, nor does Thomas Nelson vouch for the existence, content, or services of these sites, phone numbers, companies, or products beyond the life of this book.

Excerpt from *The Overcomers*, © 2024 by Matt Chandler

Note: Some names and identifying details have been changed to protect the privacy of individuals involved.

ISBN 978-1-4002-4943-5 (hardcover)
ISBN 978-1-4002-4946-6 (audiobook)
ISBN 978-1-4002-4942-8 (eBook)

Printed in Malaysia

25 26 27 28 29 OFF 10 9 8 7 6 5 4 3 2 1

TO THOSE WHO HUNGER AND
THIRST FOR RIGHTEOUSNESS:
YOU WILL BE FILLED.

CONTENTS

Introduction: Awake to a Life of Wholehearted Faith xi

DAY 1:   WAKE UP 1
DAY 2:   KNOW EXTERNAL TRUTH 6
DAY 3:   READ THE BIBLE 12
DAY 4:   SINK DEEP ROOTS 18
DAY 5:   COME ALIVE TO RELATIONSHIP 24
DAY 6:   TETHER YOURSELF TO GOD 30
DAY 7:   PURSUE INTIMACY WITH JESUS 36
DAY 8:   RECALIBRATE AS NEEDED 42
DAY 9:   GET RE-GOSPELED 48
DAY 10: SEEK ONLY JESUS 54
DAY 11: RECEIVE NEW MERCIES 60
DAY 12: COMMIT TO MORAL HOLINESS 66
DAY 13: STOP SINNING 72

DAY 14: LOVE THE FAMILY OF FAITH 78
DAY 15: BELIEVE IN THE MIRACULOUS 84
DAY 16: MATURE BY SERVING 90
DAY 17: PRAY BIG 96
DAY 18: INCREASE YOUR FAITH 102
DAY 19: ASK FOR GOD'S HELP 108
DAY 20: TRANSFORM CULTURE 114
DAY 21: BE GENEROUS 120
DAY 22: LEAVE YOUR ANXIETY WITH GOD 126
DAY 23: PLANT TREES AND LIVE FAITHFULLY 132
DAY 24: BRING YOUR SIN TO GOD 138
DAY 25: LOOSEN YOUR GRIP 144
DAY 26: REJOICE WHEN YOU REORIENT 150
DAY 27: GIVE FOR THE GOOD OF YOUR SOUL 156
DAY 28: DELIGHT IN GOD'S PRESENCE 162
DAY 29: CHOOSE WHAT MATTERS MOST 168
DAY 30: RESPOND TO GOD'S INVITATION 174

Notes 181
Acknowledgments 185
About the Author 187

INTRODUCTION

AWAKE TO A LIFE OF WHOLEHEARTED FAITH

JUNE 17 IS A big day for me every year. It's the anniversary of surrendering my life fully to King Jesus. At the time of this writing, I have just celebrated thirty-three years of His grace steadily pulling me forward. There have been seasons of great joy and awareness of His presence, and others of great hardship where I've cried out with King David, "How long, O Lord? Will you forget me forever?" (Psalm 13:1).

I write all this not knowing what season you are in as you pick up this book. I know you must be hungry to know Him and grow in your love for Him. Why else would you spend your hard-earned money on a devotional with this title? I'm glad you picked this up.

Here's my prayer for you during the next thirty days: I am praying that you

> **YOU HAVE BEEN MADE FOR A LIFE THAT REALLY IS *LIFE*.**

move more deeply into life with Jesus. When I say "life with Jesus," I mean *life*, life. The abundant life that Jesus promised in John 10:10. The fullness of life you were made for. It's waiting for you. *He* is waiting for you. You have been made for a life that really is *life*. And I'm convinced that when you purpose to embrace a life of pursuing Jesus, God will wake you up to discover a new intimacy with Him. That's what you're going to find in these pages: an invitation to know God intimately in such a way that your life is transformed.

For each day of this thirty-day challenge, we'll start with Scripture. By way of confession: I have been reading my Bible, Christian books, and devotionals for more than three decades, and I am often tempted to skip through the scriptures to get to the author's insights. Do me a favor, please: Don't do that! And be sure to ask God to open the eyes of your heart (Ephesians 1:18) as you read the living and active Word of God. Maybe some of these verses will be new to you, but I suspect that most of them will be familiar. Ask God to open your eyes to the power of His living Word.

> **ASK GOD TO OPEN THE EYES OF YOUR HEART AS YOU READ THE LIVING AND ACTIVE WORD OF GOD.**

After the daily scripture, I'll share my thoughts that I hope and pray will help you make connections between the scripture and the challenge you'll be encouraged to embrace that day. I'll invite you to reflect on what you've read, and then I'll offer you the challenge.

I really believe that if you give yourself to this experience, God will transform you from the inside out. My sincere hope is that these words will help you discover a strong foundation that equips you to experience a vibrant life of intimacy with God.

Let's do this.

DAY 1 WAKE UP

When anything is exposed by the light, it becomes visible, for anything that becomes visible is light. Therefore it says, "Awake, O sleeper, and arise from the dead, and Christ will shine on you."

EPHESIANS 5:13–14

IT WAS THREE in the morning. I was home from college, in the living room, when my little sister came running and screaming out of her bedroom. She was screaming the kind of scream that invoked pure terror in everyone else in the house. And I couldn't wake her up, despite my tackling her onto the couch. My system was flooded with adrenaline, and all the hairs on my body were standing up. She seemed to be both asleep and awake, and I was unable to snap her out of her terror.

When we sleep, our minds are moving back and forth, throughout the night, between REM cycles. And in the transition between them, weird things can happen. Somebody might sit up and start speaking. Someone else might start walking around the house.

Another person will go to the kitchen and make a sandwich. For my sister, whether it was a dark force, a repressed memory, or just some natural occurrence, in that space between being awake and being asleep, she was filled with the kind of terror that made her scream bloody murder. And all I could do was pin her to the couch.

In the fifth chapter of his letter to the church in Ephesus, Paul was concerned that the church, twelve to fifteen years after Jesus' death and resurrection, was asleep. In fact, they were so sleepy they looked almost dead. In Ephesians 5:13–14, Paul was referencing Isaiah 60:1 when he wrote: "Arise, shine, for your light has come, and the glory of the Lord has risen upon you."

Twelve to fifteen years earlier, the gospel had hit Ephesus hard. In fact, it slammed the city so hard that there had been a socioeconomic impact when people who were being transformed by Christ stopped doing economic activities that had been moneymakers for the local economy: witchcraft, temple prostitution, cultic sexual perversion, the making of idols, and more. (We'll talk a bit more about this as we go.) And in this letter Paul was saying, in essence, "Some of you have been lulled to sleep." The believers who made the decision years ago to forsake wealth for the sake of following Jesus had gotten sleepy. Like . . . *dead* sleepy.

There are two kinds of parents when waking up kids to go to school. There's that parent who comes into the room and scratches their kid's back, cooing, "Hey, sweetie. I know it's early; I know. We need you to get up, babe. You got this. We just gotta get you dressed." Then there's that other parent who barks, "I need you up, *now*! I've got things I'm working on, so get up because I got stuff to do!" Well, when Paul was writing to the church in Ephesus, in an attempt to wake them up, he was not bringing gentle, scratch-your-back Jesus. It was more, "Hey! The house is on fire! Get up! You're going to die! Get out *now*!"

This letter to the church in Ephesus wasn't for unbelievers. Paul wasn't inviting them to wake up and come to life. No, this message was for followers of Christ. It's for followers of Christ today as well. And what I believe God wants to do in you is wake you up. Whether you've been snoozing or are knocked out cold, God is waking you up by His Spirit.

So my sister Heather was on the couch, screaming in her sleep. I was screaming, too, out of my own terror and also to wake her, but I couldn't get my voice to work. I'd never seen her like this before, and I was filled with fear because she wouldn't wake up and she wouldn't stop screaming. But I guess this must've been happening for a while, and my mom knew what was going on that night. Suddenly, I heard my mom's door open. She walked over to Heather, gently said her name, and Heather woke up.

HAVE YOU FALLEN ASLEEP?

Have you fallen asleep? Maybe you're mad at God because of something that happened to you. Maybe you feel like God betrayed you. Or maybe *nothing* happened to you, but you got really sluggish along the way and fell asleep. There might've been some soft music and cozy chairs that hypnotized you. If you're half asleep, I want you to have the courage to name it.

Let's wake up. Don't let the deceiver trick you. Let's get going and wake up!

REFLECT

1. Remember where your journey with God began. When was the moment in your spiritual journey in which you felt most fully alive and awake?

2. Have you experienced a "wake-up" call from God in any area of your life? How have you experienced God's Spirit shining light on an area of your life in such a way that it woke you up spiritually?

CHALLENGE

In his letter to the church in Ephesus, Paul reminded them, "But when anything is exposed by the light, it becomes visible" (5:13). Sleepy friend, that's what God does. God shines light on the areas of our lives to which we've squeezed our eyes shut. God makes these places—our habits, neglect, sin, laziness—visible. Ask God to show you the areas of your life He wants to touch and transform. Today, ask Him to show you just one thing, and then record it someplace: a note on the mirror, in your phone, or in your journal.

DAY 2
KNOW EXTERNAL TRUTH

"Let not your hearts be troubled. Believe in God; believe also in me. In my Father's house are many rooms. If it were not so, would I have told you that I go to prepare a place for you? And if I go and prepare a place for you, I will come again and will take you to myself, that where I am you may be also. And you know the way to where I am going." Thomas said to him, "Lord, we do not know where you are going. How can we know the way?" Jesus said to him, "I am the way, and the truth, and the life. No one comes to the Father except through me."

JOHN 14:1–6

IT WAS 1992. It was one of the most watched court cases in American history. Tom Cruise—I mean, Lieutenant Daniel Kaffee—is defending Lance Corporal Harold Dawson and Private First-Class Louden Downey, who stand accused of the murder of a fellow marine, Private First-Class William Santiago. They are facing murder charges as well as a court martial. As the investigation progresses, it becomes clear that although Dawson and Downey are guilty, they are acting on an order given to them by a commanding officer—an order that they would not have been able to *not* obey.

> **FACTS AND TRUTH AREN'T THE SAME.**

So Tom Cruise puts Colonel Nathan Jessup (Jack Nicholson) on the stand and grills him.

"Colonel Jessup, did you order the code red?"

The judge jumps in: "You don't have to answer that question."

Nicholson says, "I'll answer the question. You want answers?"

Tom Cruise says, "I think I'm entitled to them."

"You want answers?" Nicholson repeats.

"I want the truth!" Cruise demands.

Then Nicholson, from his bowels, roars, "You can't handle the truth!"[1]

It. Was. Epic.

Then they get into it. Go watch *A Few Good Men.* It holds up.

What I think ended up happening is that they were talking about facts under the banner of truth. You understand? Facts and truth aren't the same. Facts are things we can see, touch, taste, smell, and hear. Truth is what sits beneath those things and orients us to reality. So facts may point to a specific time, place, or action, but truth is behind all those facts, saying, "This is what the universe is all about."

There's another well-known court case where Jesus was arrested and taken to an authority named Pontius Pilate. Pilate didn't want to kill Jesus, but he lacked the courage to live a life of conviction. In John 18:37–38, Pilate said to Jesus, in essence, "You're a king." Jesus answered, "You say that I'm a king. In fact, the reason I was born and came into the world is to testify to the truth. Everyone on the side of truth listens to Me." And Pilate asked, "What is truth?"

Do you see how they were missing each other? Pilate was jammed up on facts, and the Truth was standing right in front of him.

Before this, Jesus' disciples were already getting anxious at Jesus' talk about death, about being arrested. It had been disorienting. They didn't understand what He was saying to them. In John 14:1–4, Jesus said to His closest friends, "Let not your hearts be troubled. Believe in God; believe also in me. In my Father's house are many rooms. If it were not so, would I have told you that I go to prepare a place for you? And if I go and prepare a place for you, I will come again and will take you to myself, that where I am you may be also. And you know the way to where I am going."

> **JESUS *IS* THE TRUTH. IT'S NOT SOMETHING THAT HE *HAS*.**

I love Thomas's response. In verse 5, Thomas basically said, "We literally have no idea what You're talking about."

And then Jesus answered him, "I am the way, and the truth, and the life. No one comes to the Father except through me" (v. 6).

Jesus *is* the truth. It's not something that He *has*. He's not here to give you some facts. He has come because He is

8 | AWAKE AND ALIVE

reality. He's not just a good teacher. He's ultimate reality. He's not just a miracle worker; He is the truth. He sets boundaries for human flourishing, and then He invites us in. He makes a way for all our enemies to be vanquished—especially the enemy of sin that's inside of us. He isn't the facts of life. He *orders* the facts of life.

He is the truth, and He *is* what you and I most want. Right? We want to know the way. We want purpose. We want a life that's flourishing. And those are inseparably linked to Jesus as ultimate reality. Jesus is the eternal, unchanging truth, present from the time of creation, available to every individual who seeks it.

REFLECT

1. How does the distinction between *facts* and *truth* resonate with you? Does it make sense?

   _____
   _____
   _____
   _____
   _____
   _____
   _____

2. In your life, how have you known Jesus as the way, the truth, and the life (John 14:6)?

   _____
   _____
   _____
   _____
   _____
   _____
   _____

CHALLENGE

This is another fun one. Jesus makes Himself known to His closest disciples as the way, the truth, and the life. I encourage you to choose one of the first three Gospels and read through it starting today, asking God to illumine these truths as you read: in Jesus' relationships, in His words, in His actions. You're not looking at the minutiae of facts about Jesus; you're recognizing Him for how He reveals Himself in larger ways as the way, as the truth, and as the life. Spend time getting to know Him. Consider recording in a journal what you notice as you read and pray.

DAY 3 READ THE BIBLE

In the beginning was the Word, and the Word was with God, and the Word was God. He was in the beginning with God. All things were made through him, and without him was not any thing made that was made. In him was life, and the life was the light of men. The light shines in the darkness, and the darkness has not overcome it.

JOHN 1:1–5

WHEN SARAH MET Christ in college, she was fired up to love Him and be loved by Him. Every morning she woke up at 5:30 to spend time in His Word and in prayer. She kept a journal where she'd record all that she was praying for, and she'd leave notes, weeks or months later, when God answered those prayers. If her school or work schedule changed, she'd adjust her day to make room to spend intimate time with God.

When Sarah arrived at graduate school—graduate school to

prepare for *ministry*—she reasoned that she was reading the Bible for classes and to write papers and take quizzes, so that was probably the same thing as being with God just to be in His presence. Probably.

Only . . . it wasn't. Five years after Sarah met Christ, no one who saw her would have guessed that she'd withered spiritually. When she showed up in church wearing a cute outfit and a smile, it was impossible to tell that the only time Sarah was reading the Bible was when her preacher asked the congregation to open up to a particular passage. At first, she was still carrying her Bible to church. Eventually, though, she'd go through the motions, as if she was opening the Bible app on her phone, but she'd just check texts as the church's faulty reception allowed.

God's Word is the food we need to flourish in this world. And God wants you to know truth. He hasn't hidden it. He hasn't put it in places where you can't find it. He didn't put it on the top shelf. No, God wants you to know the truth. He wants you to know and see ultimate reality for what it is so that the facts of your life might lead to purpose and flourishing. So that the facts of your life won't lead to chaos, heartbreak, loneliness, despair, and deep brokenness.

The primary way that you and I get to see and know and understand the truth is in the revelation of God and His purposes and plans in the Scriptures. The

> **GOD'S WORD IS THE FOOD WE NEED TO FLOURISH IN THIS WORLD.**

READ THE BIBLE | 13

Bible is about God revealing to us the truth of who He is. We are people of the Book.

Scripture is a miraculous book. It's a truth book. It has sixty-six books penned by forty different authors across fifteen hundred years and three continents. *One story*. The Bible, from Genesis to Revelation, tells the same story. It's the story of God redeeming and saving people, His creation, from the brokenness of death. It starts in Genesis, and it ends in Revelation.

> **THE BIBLE IS A MIRACULOUS BOOK TELLING ONE STORY.**

There are seven main genres in the Scriptures. There are the books of the law. Then there are the books of history. There are the books of poetry and wisdom literature. The prophets are there to warn and encourage us. There are letters. And there are the Gospels. Many times when people attack the Bible, trying to undermine its authority, they take something out of genre and make a big deal out of it. They might take a poem or a song and malign it as if it were something other than what it is. They'll critique it as if it's a history book. It's not. Or they'll read something specific to ancient Near Eastern culture through a modern ideological framework. That will break your brain.

The Bible is a miraculous book telling one story. None of these authors met over coffee to discuss what they were writing. There was no human lead editor or project manager on this thing. There was the Holy Spirit. That's it.

So how did they write it? Well, they wrote it with reed pens and ink. They wrote it using their own hands and their own minds. Humans wrote the Bible. If anybody ever says that—likely as an accusation—know that it's absolutely true. Men wrote the Bible, inspired by the Holy Spirit.

And because I know that there is life in the words of Scripture, I will, at times, become frustrated by the sheer volume of propaganda that's trying to take from you—*violently* take from you—how miraculous this book is, how powerful it could be for you.

The Bible is how God reveals Himself as the truth, as ultimate reality, to you and to me.

God wants you to know that truth has moved toward you in the person of Jesus and has revealed Himself fully to you in the scriptures. So we're people of the Book: informed by, shaped by, and submitting to God's revelation in and through it. And we're living boldly by its decrees and its commands.

The Bible itself must not ever become a textbook for evaluation. Rather, it is the pathway to see God as He really is. Brother, sister, what might change in your life if you said, "Holy Spirit, help me see the beauty of Jesus and You"?

REFLECT

1. How would you describe your relationship with God's Word over the course of your life with Him?

_____
_____
_____
_____
_____
_____
_____

2. Today, are you steeped in the goodness of God's Word? Why or why not?

_____
_____
_____
_____
_____
_____
_____

CHALLENGE

John opened His gospel by announcing who Jesus is. He was in the beginning, and now He's arrived on the scene. Chapter by chapter, verse by verse, I want you to soak yourself in John's Gospel, starting today. Discover Jesus in this rich telling of His birth, life, ministry, death, resurrection, and ascension. Read it as if you're discovering everything there is to know about a new friend. Ask the Holy Spirit to encourage your heart by the beauty of Jesus that you see there. Ask Him to orient your heart around Jesus as the ultimate reality of the universe and of your life.

DAY 4: SINK DEEP ROOTS

"Hear then the parable of the sower: . . . As for what was sown on rocky ground, this is the one who hears the word and immediately receives it with joy, yet he has no root in himself, but endures for a while, and when tribulation or persecution arises on account of the word, immediately he falls away."

MATTHEW 13:18, 20–21

IF YOU HAD to make a list of classic rom-coms, which films would you include? I want you to think of some Hollywood pairing, a couple in love, and picture this man and woman in your mind. And then I want to ask you a question: How old are the individuals? I'm going to take a shot in the dark and say that when we think of romantic love, couples who are crazy about each other, we often think of the romantic love shared between individuals during the first few decades of life.

Whether it's a Disney Princess or some new streaming rom-com, this kind of love is superemotional. These lovers are starry-eyed. And those stars can interfere with their vision, right? Because in this kind of sentimental, romantic love, the guy or the girl can't see any fault in the other person. It's awesome. It's easy. We love it.

In his epic book on prayer, *Praying Like Monks, Living Like Fools*, Tyler Staton, a pastor in Portland, names this kind of romantic love "young love." But he also points to a different kind of love, and that's "old love."[1] I'm not going to lie; I love it when I'm out on the street and see a couple like this. This is the couple in their eighties who are still holding hands, and they're crazy about each other. But we don't see that as much, do we? We don't see it on-screen very often, and we don't see it out in the streets. It's the kind of relationship that has deep roots, and it's rare.

> **THE DEEP-ROOTED LIFE WITH CHRIST, THE ROBUST POWER OF THE GOSPEL, IS AVAILABLE TO THOSE WHO WILL GO AFTER IT.**

When the lives of Jesus' earliest followers were first turned upside down by the power of the gospel, they were like that starry-eyed young couple in love. And Jesus acknowledged that even many of those listening to Him teach while He was alive wouldn't keep that lovin' feeling. They wouldn't stay the course (Matthew 24:10). He knew they wouldn't become that couple who was still in love after fifty or sixty years of marriage. But He also knows that it's possible. It's

SINK DEEP ROOTS | 19

available to us. The deep-rooted life with Christ, the robust power of the gospel, is available to those who will go after it.

In the parable of the sower in Matthew 13, the Greek word *petra* Jesus used for the seed thrown on rocky ground literally means that when tribulations come, when the believer's faith is tested, they not only fall away, but they also have contempt in their hearts. Maybe you know someone like this. When bad things happen, they get angry with God. Maybe they encountered Jesus in a real way ten or fifteen years ago. They fell on the ground, recognized their sin, and begged Jesus to save them. Their lives were transformed. At first, they probably looked like they were thriving. They changed the kinds of music they were listening to. They woke up at 4 a.m. every day for prayer. They cried during worship. They felt all of it. But their roots didn't sink deep. They weren't grounded. They were, essentially, rootless.

Friend, when those tribulations come, there's a better way. Because when a child gets sick, when a marriage is on the rocks, when a job is at risk, you can lean into God's provision. God doesn't promise that we won't have pain; He promises to be with us in our pain. In our anger. In our fear. If you haven't been there, it's coming. If you have been there, there's more coming. Sorry.

C. S. Lewis wrote, "Relying on God has to begin all over again every day as if nothing had yet been done."[2] It's true, but it's not original to Lewis. The Word says that God's mercies are new every morning (Lamentations 3:22–23). Praise God. Let's get after it today. Let's go again tomorrow.

Maybe yesterday you were in the Word. You prayed. You clung to the Lord. You walked out life with your Christian friends. You made it. Praise God. But let's go again tomorrow. His mercies are new, and the tank will be filled in the morning.

We weren't made for shallow faith. We weren't made for flimsy, starry-eyed faith that crashes and burns after three months. We were made for the long journey home. You can choose to grow your roots deep so that when tribulation comes your way—not *if*, but *when*—you can hold fast.

> **WE WEREN'T MADE FOR SHALLOW FAITH.**

REFLECT

1. Think of a couple who has that "old love" endurance in their relationship. What would you guess is the secret sauce in their relationship?

_____

_____

_____

_____

_____

2. In what ways have you been intentional about nourishing your life with God so that you are developing deep roots?

_____

_____

_____

_____

_____

CHALLENGE

Consistency is boring. It is. I wake up at five a.m. and open my Bible at our kitchen island. And you know how many times the Spirit has overwhelmed me in that moment? The numbers aren't strong. But every once in a while—and He's always doing this whether I know it or not—He'll expand my capacity for endurance. It's what He does. He expands our capacity for endurance. He expands our capacity for intimacy. The challenge for today is to commit to sinking your roots deep by making time to spend with God daily. Put it on your calendar, schedule it to repeat, and keep that appointment.

DAY 5: COME ALIVE TO RELATIONSHIP

"I am the true vine, and my Father is the vinedresser. Every branch in me that does not bear fruit he takes away, and every branch that does bear fruit he prunes, that it may bear more fruit. Already you are clean because of the word that I have spoken to you. Abide in me, and I in you. As the branch cannot bear fruit by itself, unless it abides in the vine, neither can you, unless you abide in me. I am the vine; you are the branches. Whoever abides in me and I in him, he it is that bears much fruit, for apart from me you can do nothing."

JOHN 15:1–5

NOT TOO LONG ago, I did a funeral for a woman named Jane Thompson. She was eighty-two years old when she went home to be with the Lord. And at eighty-two, she was still hosting a gathering of young adults in her home every week. She simply refused to get crusty as she aged. She refused to look at the next generation as something to lament but rather as an opportunity to herald the majesty of Jesus. But there's so much more to Jane's story.

Jane was adopted as a child into a fundamentalist Christian home. And when I say *fundamentalist*, you've got to take the "f-u-n" out of that. There was no dancing. No secular music. And while there may be latent wisdom in some of that, the problem was that it was a checklist of rules. You likely know what I mean about viewing Christianity as a

> **YOU LIKELY KNOW WHAT I MEAN ABOUT VIEWING CHRISTIANITY AS A CHECKLIST RATHER THAN A LIVING, VIBRANT LOVE RELATIONSHIP.**

checklist rather than a living, vibrant love relationship. And Jane grew up with the checklist. You couldn't go to a dance, but you could put on skates and go dance on wheels at the skating rink on Friday night. You were dancing, but you just weren't calling it that. It's that kind of weird hypocrisy that always tends to follow fundamentalism. Well, that's what she grew up in. And she was good at it.

So she got engaged to Bob during her senior year of high school. (It was a different era!) She received the ring at graduation. She and Bob were both in this stream of fundamentalism. By the time Jane was thirty-eight, she was a deacon's wife. She was playing the piano at church. She was winning at *church*.

One Sunday, though, after Jane played the piano, she went and sat down with the rest of the congregation. The pastor was preaching the message at this small church, and in the middle of his sermon, Jane heard this whisper say, *You don't know Me.* It was the Holy Spirit. The voice continued, *You know about Me, but you don't know Me.*

What I love is that it made her angry.

And she talked back, explaining to Jesus why He was so wrong.

She spat this epically long list: "I play the piano. I'm a deacon's wife. I don't cuss, drink, or smoke. I don't tolerate those who do."

The Spirit whispered again, *But you don't know Me.*

Then Jane did one of the gutsiest things I've ever heard. That afternoon, she went home and opened up the Gospel of Luke. And she wrestled with Jesus in the Gospel of Luke. And by the middle of the afternoon, she was like, "Dang it. I'm not a Christian."

Is that gritty or what?

Buckle up, because it's not over.

She went back to church that same Sunday night. (You gotta be really old to remember Sunday night church. It's a whole different service on Sunday night. Count 'em: *two!*) So she was playing the piano, and at the end, when the pastor invited anyone who wanted to know Jesus to come to the front and pray for salvation, she was moved to go to the front. She tried to rationalize it away, telling herself and telling God, "But I teach the youth, and they're here. They're not going to understand. Come on, God; I'm playing the piano. It's going to be really weird."

And the Spirit said, *Let's go, Jane.*

The preacher said, "If you want to become a Christian, come on up here."

In obedience, Jane stopped playing the piano. And now it was dead silent. And she walked out from behind the piano and walked up to the pastor in front of everybody who assumed she was a mature believer. And then she gave her life to Jesus for the first time. She accepted Christ as a thirty-eight-year-old deacon's wife who played piano at church. And at her funeral, nine grandchildren testified about G-ma's faithfulness as the root of their own faith.

I'm curious what you think of Jane's story. Personally, I think it's incredible. And I also think it's rare. I think there are a lot of spiritually dead folks out in the pews, and I think Jane has shown us the good way. I think her willingness to say yes—albeit a reluctant *yes!*—gives us a glimpse of what God wants to do in lives like ours. In religious lives. In those of us who are churchy. God is calling us, but a lot of us don't have Jane's courage. A part of us *does* know that we're not connected to Jesus, we're not attached to the vine, but we silence the part that knows. We hear the Spirit whispering, inviting us into an intimate relationship with Jesus. But rather than get off the piano bench and meet Him for ourselves, we'd rather (in our pride) keep playing the part.

SAY YES.

Beloved, if the Holy Spirit is whispering to you that you know *about* Jesus but you don't know Him, take courage, for the Spirit is calling your name.

Say yes.

REFLECT

1. How is Jane's story unlike your story? How is Jane's story like your story? What does that mean for you today?

_____

_____

_____

_____

_____

_____

2. If Jesus is the vine, and you are a branch, what does your connection to Him look like today? What's the fruit?

_____

_____

_____

_____

_____

_____

CHALLENGE

In John 15:1, Jesus identifies Himself as the "true vine." And the invitation, to me and to you, is to be connected to that vine. If we're not, we die. His specific invitation is, "Abide in me, and I in you" (v. 4). Today, I want you to be as gutsy and honest as you've ever been. Pay attention to the part of you that may know how connected or disconnected you are to Him today. Let God's Spirit speak to your heart. Specifically, prayerfully, imagine the garden of your heart. Let the Vinedresser show you the condition of your heart's garden, and ask Him how you are to tend to it. Listen.

DAY 6
TETHER YOURSELF TO GOD

For this reason I bow my knees before the Father, from whom every family in heaven and on earth is named, that according to the riches of his glory he may grant you to be strengthened with power through his Spirit in your inner being, so that Christ may dwell in your hearts through faith—that you, being rooted and grounded in love, may have strength to comprehend with all the saints what is the breadth and length and height and depth, and to know the love of Christ that surpasses knowledge, that you may be filled with all the fullness of God.

EPHESIANS 3:14–19

DURING THE PAST two decades, I have traveled enough to get significant status on my preferred airline. That means I have been delayed, canceled, and spent more of my life than I'd like to admit in an airport terminal. One of my favorite things to do in an airport is people-watch. It doesn't take long to spot the differences between the business travelers who've been on the road longer than they'd like and the newbies who are trying to navigate through the herd of people. I have also watched the tearstained faces of those who are traveling toward some destination that isn't a beach vacation. I've even watched seemingly normal people completely lose their minds with airline employees because something didn't go the way they expected.

If you keep your eyes open in an airport, you're also going to see some amazing things. You'll start seeing infants, toddlers, and children. (I won't lie; they're much cuter in the terminal than when they're seated right behind you on the plane at full volume.)

Invariably, you're going to see a parent walking through the terminal with an infant strapped to their chest. You've seen these baby carriers, right? When they're walking toward you, you'll see a little head below the parent's head. And if the baby is old enough, maybe six to nine months, they're facing forward. So there will also be four floppy limbs bouncing happily along as the mom or dad walks the three miles to Terminal Gate E38. The parents might be exhausted, but the baby? The baby is golden. She needs nothing because she's tethered to her parent. I guarantee you that anything that little one could possibly need is in the diaper bag on the mom or dad's shoulder. That baby feels completely secure.

On more than one occasion, that picture has reminded me of my relationship with God. It's hard for me to imagine myself as an infant tethered to his father's body, but it's true, and it's what we were made for. Did you know that that's what God's after? Did you know that that's available to you as a son or a daughter of God?

> TOO OFTEN, WE GET IT WRONG, ESPECIALLY WHEN WE'VE BEEN CHURCHY FOR A LONG TIME.

Too often, we get it wrong, especially when we've been churchy for a long time. If we grew up in the church, or if we've been around it for a while, we can act as if our faith is about an ever-increasing knowledge of God. Or it's about maintaining a standard of behavior that we can't possibly maintain. No, that's not what we're made for. We were made to have security, provision, and intimacy with God.

And our faith is rooted in an understanding of God's love that keeps us tethered to Him.

That's not to say we won't try to do all the things, know all the things, and be all the things. Yet when we try to get God to validate our list of the things we think we should do, He says, *No, just be with Me. Be with Me.*

It's a little mind-bending, isn't it?

In this world where we're measured by our test scores and sales numbers, it's slightly disorienting. It's a little confusing. We're not quite sure what to do with the caregiver who loves us and isn't hustling us to get out the door in the morning. Or nagging us to pick up our rooms. Or to walk the dog. Or to do the dishes. We're not used to the one who loves us inviting us to just *be*. To just be with Him.

And to be fair, most of us didn't have moms or dads like that. After all, they had stuff to do! If anyone tells me they had perfect parents, I know they're wrong. They might want to believe that, but the reality is none of us was raised by perfect humans because perfect humans simply do not exist. Case closed. None of us has experienced perfect love in our childhood home, dorm room, or home we live in today. We just haven't. And we're so broken that when we finally taste the real thing, it feels disingenuous.

No, we protest. *It can't be true.*

We're the prodigal son coming home after living it up in the streets, and the Father spots us at a distance and runs to our side. And He is *elated* that we're there.

It's as if He's saying, "You're home!" And inviting us even closer, saying, "Root yourself in My love. I'm right here. I'm so committed. I'm committed to you with My broken body and blood. I'm here for you. I want you. I want you for the long haul."

If the prodigal son's dad could scoop up his twenty-something kid and tether him to his middle-aged chest, he would. And that's a picture of how our heavenly Father straps us close and provides everything we need. He tethers the grieving daughter close to His heart. He'll even bind the outraged passenger who needs to be soothed.

You were made to be planted and rooted and tethered and grounded in the steadfast love of a Father who does not fail.

REFLECT

1. Imagine you're that kid at the airport with a parent. Are you running circles through the terminal? Are you crouched someplace, hiding? Are you bundled against the body of a parent who is safe, trustworthy, and kind? Where are you?

_____
_____
_____
_____
_____

2. Spend time imagining your heavenly Parent whose deep desire is to welcome you near and hold you close. Do you believe it? Do you welcome it? Or do you have some reservations?

_____
_____
_____
_____
_____

CHALLENGE

My prayer for you as you embrace today's challenge is the same as Paul's prayer for the early believers in Ephesus: "That you, being rooted and grounded in love, may have strength to comprehend with all the saints what is the breadth and length and height and depth, and to know the love of Christ that surpasses knowledge" (3:17–19). I want you to know in your deepest places the wide, long, high, deep love of Christ. Today, I encourage you to quiet your heart in prayer and see yourself tethered to the Father who loves you. Ask Him, "Show me how wide, how long, how high, and how deep Your love is for me." Then wait. Be patient. Let the Spirit speak to your heart. Repeat as needed.

DAY 7
PURSUE INTIMACY WITH JESUS

"What woman, having ten silver coins, if she loses one coin, does not light a lamp and sweep the house and seek diligently until she finds it? And when she has found it, she calls together her friends and neighbors, saying, 'Rejoice with me, for I have found the coin that I had lost.' Just so, I tell you, there is joy before the angels of God over one sinner who repents."

LUKE 15:8–10

"DID I ACTUALLY surrender my life to Jesus?"

I was at a Starbucks with this thirty-something guy, and as he shared his story with me, he was crying. Not just teary-eyed; I mean snot and tears. He was ugly crying. It was the kind of situation where you might be embarrassed to be sitting across from that. (Not me, of course, but some people would.) And this young man was wrestling through whether his conversion at age eight was real. Was it his own or was it for his mom? Because in his teen and young adult years, he'd had some pretty epic failures—the kind where a lot of churches are not going to welcome you in.

As I listened, I began to understand what we are up against in the Bible Belt. Too many churches are more concerned about your behavior than whether you have a life-giving relationship with Jesus. Maybe this has been your experience too.

And it wasn't just this one young man. Countless twenty- and thirty-somethings tell me, with a straight face, that they grew up in church, participated in vacation Bible school, went to youth camp—and *they never heard the gospel.* They knew what they should and shouldn't do, they knew the morality of the kingdom, but they knew nothing of intimacy with Jesus.

And this man who was sipping a grande caffè mocha between his sobs was asking, "Did I actually surrender my life to Jesus when I was eight? Or was I just trying to please my mom?"

I *do* believe that an eight-year-old can surrender to Jesus and fall in love with Him, because that's my wife's story. Her faith has grown, but she'd be the first to tell you of her eight-year-old self, "I knew Him. I loved Him. I was crazy about Him." Her faith was, and is, real.

But what I am seeing and hearing is that many in the church have a misunderstanding—like these young people I was encountering—of what it means to know and love God.

I'll bet you know folks like this. And it's also possible that you *are* someone like this. If that's you, I want you to own it. Or have you fallen asleep? Have you fallen under a spell? Have you, in some way, been lulled to sleep? Because you are a son or daughter who was created for relationship with the King.

If this is your story, if you've been sleeping, then the Holy Spirit might be waking you up today. Your story might be like the story of this young man. Maybe your faith *was* sincere, but because you weren't attached to the vine and bore no fruit, you're wondering if it was real. You want authentic life in Him, but you took a wrong turn.

> **IF YOU'VE BEEN SLEEPING, THEN THE HOLY SPIRIT MIGHT BE WAKING YOU UP TODAY.**

It may also be possible that your story is just the opposite of this guy's story. Maybe you've been working really hard religiously but have never surrendered and had a relationship with Jesus. Different tune, same song. Even if you've been showing up at church, your heart might be just as far from Jesus, in this moment, as the man who was undone in the café that day. I hope you can sense my tone in these words: *I'm not condemning you.* I'm just checking in to see if you're sleepy. Because if you are, I want to invite you into the joy and vitality of awake life in Jesus.

If your heart is far from Jesus today, in any variety of circumstances, you are that lost coin described in Luke 15 that Jesus has been hunting for. I mean, He's turned on His cell phone flashlight; He's breathing in the dust from under the beds because He's looking for you. And what He has for you now is so much better than whatever was happening where you were hiding from Him. It's intimacy. He's welcoming you into a loving relationship with Him.

It doesn't matter if you first met Christ when you were eight, eighteen, or eighty-eight. What matters is whether you're experiencing that intimacy for which you were made. That's the love relationship my wife has known with Christ. Or are you heartbroken, like the man across the table from me at Starbucks? Have you missed out on some good years of intimacy with Christ because of either irreligiosity or religiosity? More importantly, will that grief you feel move you into the relationship with Him for which you were made?

Today, you can say yes to it—yes to intimacy with Christ.

REFLECT

1. When you think of these two temptations—the temptation to choose sin and flee from God, or the temptation to hide in plain sight at church—which one is closer to your story? How?

   _____
   _____
   _____
   _____
   _____
   _____

2. On a scale from 1 to 10, how heartbroken are you about the distance you've created between you and God? Notice that and offer it to God.

   _____
   _____
   _____
   _____
   _____
   _____

CHALLENGE

I'm inviting you to ask the question of yourself that matters more than any other: "Do I have an intimate relationship with God through Jesus Christ?" I hope the answer is yes. If it's not, today is a great opportunity for you to begin a life-giving relationship with the One who loves you. I'll offer a prayer you can pray. And if you do have a relationship with Jesus, I encourage you to pray this prayer, making it your own. Speak to God from your heart. All you need is a heart posture that is open to intimacy with God. You can pray something like this:

Father, stir up belief in my heart through Your Spirit. Give me courage to develop the kind of intimacy with You that represents the life I was made for. I hear Your voice calling me today, and my answer is yes. I want to know You for myself—face-to-face, voice-to-voice, heart-to-heart. I confess that, even if I've been in church a long time, I've never really heard or understood this idea of an intimate relationship with You. Thank You for waking me up to You and Your presence. I lay all this at Your feet. Do what only You can do. In Your beautiful name I pray, amen.

DAY 8 RECALIBRATE AS NEEDED

"I have loved you," says the Lord. But you say, "How have you loved us?" "Is not Esau Jacob's brother?" declares the Lord. "Yet I have loved Jacob but Esau I have hated. I have laid waste his hill country and left his heritage to jackals of the desert." If Edom says, "We are shattered but we will rebuild the ruins," the Lord of hosts says, "They may build, but I will tear down, and they will be called 'the wicked country,' and 'the people with whom the Lord is angry forever.'" Your own eyes shall see this, and you shall say, "Great is the Lord beyond the border of Israel!"

MALACHI 1:2—5

YOU KNOW WHEN your life is on fire.

If a significant relationship in your life has just ended, you may be struggling to hear God's voice today. If the IRS is breathing down your neck, you may not be *feeling* God's love. If your heart is broken, you may be raising your fist at God, whom you're struggling to see through the smoky wreckage.

In moments like these, we may naturally long for comfort from the false gods of our making: Butler Jesus, or Genie-in-a-Lamp Jesus, or Tinker Bell Jesus, who sprinkles fairy dust that makes everything better. We create these convenient, costumed gods when we handpick verses from the Bible—the ones that make us feel warm and fuzzy inside when we see them on a bumper sticker or a greeting card. But the reality is that the Bible tells *one story*. The sixty-six books of the Bible form a singular story of God interacting with His people. So how do we reconcile a God who we know is good—but maybe not "genie" good—with the carnage and chaos we see in the Bible and in our lives?

This hard message in Malachi can actually help.

What we're glimpsing in the book of Malachi is an absolute train wreck of a moment in the history of God's people. (At the same time, it may not sound so different from what we see in our world today!) Although God's people had been brought out of slavery and into the promised land, they'd forgotten about the God who saved them. There was pervasive religious skepticism in the community. There was moral deterioration and religious apathy. The nation's institutions—both the government and the Church—were inept; they were corrupt. The people were suffering from severe poverty due to Persian economic policies. And in the midst of this big mess, God sent His prophet Malachi to invite people to return to the Lord.

God's word through Malachi, in chapter 1, began the same way that all God's interactions with us begin. In the midst of our mess, God's posture toward us is one of love. And in the midst of *their* mess, God led by saying, in essence, "I love you now, and I'll love you forever." If you've never read the book of Malachi yet something about that sounds familiar, it's because it resonates with Paul's insistence in Romans 5:8, where he announced that *"while we were still sinners*, Christ died for us." This is who God is. God loves us *before* we ever get it together. That's the order God chose. He delivered His people out of slavery and *then* He gave them the Law, coaching them in how life should be ordered. It was redemption first and then holiness.

So when God announced His love through Malachi, what was the response of His children? They asked, "How have you loved us?" (v. 2). That's us, right? We are the whiny children. When we've chosen to go our own way, to drive off and do our own thing, and we end up in a ditch, God invites us to look toward Him. And from the ditch we see a God who has promised not to destroy us, as He's destroyed others, but whose steadfast love and justice do not fail.

> **WE ARE THE WHINY CHILDREN.**

But can we just go back, for a moment, to how you got into the ditch? If you have no idea, I'm going to suggest that—like the Israelites—you may have gone rogue when it came to doing things God's way. Maybe it involved money. Maybe it was around sexuality. Every time we turn our back on the way God has designed us and the love He's called us into, we become more and more dehumanized. We live in ways that cause chaos and hurt and pain and death and sorrow and sadness. Yet when we finally surrender—fully surrender—to the love of Christ made available to us in the gospel, we at last become more and more who and what we're meant to be.

The place God began with the Israelites, in their mess, is where God begins with us: *I have loved you.*

Whether you're in the ditch today, or you've got your foot on the gas to end up there, God is inviting you to slow down, pivot, and return to Him. To experience His love anew. Maybe you'll feel warm and fuzzy inside, and maybe you won't. But there are practical steps God outlined for Israel that will serve you well today. I encourage you to read the entire book of Malachi, but for now read the threefold prescription God gave through Malachi for the people of Israel:

1. Renew your commitment to God's instruction, especially when it comes to worship.
2. Practice loyalty to covenants, especially marriage.
3. Steward your material possessions faithfully, especially when it comes to hoarding and sharing.

The hearts of the Israelites were exactly like our hearts. So I'm wondering: What's the mess in which you find yourself today? Where are you stuck? As you make the decision to align your life with God's good design, as you turn your face to receive His love, the One who loved you from the beginning will receive you and transform you.

REFLECT

1. Spend time with God's promise, "I have loved you." Reflect on what this promise stirs up in your mind and emotions as you sit with it. Grab a journal and make a list of the moments in your life when you *experienced* God's love.

_____

_____

_____

_____

2. How have you been stuck or how have you suffered—either today or in the past—because you turned your back on God's good design? Practice being quiet and let God's Spirit guide you as you reflect.

_____

_____

_____

_____

CHALLENGE

In response to God's love, what is the *one thing* God is asking of you in this moment as you are waking up to become who you were made to be? Maybe God is asking you to give up something: a destructive habit, relationship, or something else. Or maybe God is asking you to take a particular action, either with a hard conversation or other assignment you'd prefer to avoid. Be specific about the way you'll respond to God's instruction to you today.

DAY 9
GET RE-GOSPELED

I am astonished that you are so quickly deserting him who called you in the grace of Christ and are turning to a different gospel—not that there is another one, but there are some who trouble you and want to distort the gospel of Christ. But even if we or an angel from heaven should preach to you a gospel contrary to the one we preached to you, let him be accursed. As we have said before, so now I say again: If anyone is preaching to you a gospel contrary to the one you received, let him be accursed.

GALATIANS 1:6–9

OVER THE PAST twenty years, I've heard young adults tell me that although they grew up in church, went to vacation Bible school, and were active in their church's youth ministry, it wasn't until they started attending The Village Church that they actually heard the gospel. I have almost always been skeptical of this narrative. More often than not, when they return home to visit their parents and friends and go back to their home church, they are surprised to hear their old pastor preaching the gospel faithfully.

This is what God does. The Holy Spirit quickens our hearts, wakes us up, if we've never really surrendered and never had a relationship with Jesus. That enlivening is what the Spirit does.

A lot of times, when we're reading the Bible, we think it sounds like good stuff. We might even think of a relative or a coworker who doesn't know Christ who could really benefit from what we're reading in God's Word. And we might evenly pray *earnestly* for that person to wake up and come alive in Christ.

Unfortunately, many of us believe and behave like the gospel is for unbelievers. But what's striking is that most of the time the gospel is proclaimed in the New Testament, it's proclaimed to Christians, not non-Christians.[1] You getting that? But we've flipped it. We've made it a door that sinners can walk through

> **YOU AND I ARE IN DESPERATE NEED TO REPEATEDLY BE RE-GOSPELED AND TO UNDERSTAND IT AND WALK IN IT.**

and then we don't have to worry anymore. But that's not how the Bible presents the gospel. The Bible says that you and I are in desperate need to repeatedly be re-gospeled and to understand it and walk in it. Because we're prone to forget it. We're prone to drift away.

And that's why, in his letter to the Galatians, Paul went hard. You know how he started some of his letters all touchy-feely? "Grace and peace to you. Love you. Hope you're doing well." Well, this is *not* the tone of Galatians.

In Galatians 1:6, Paul called them out: "I am astonished that you are so quickly deserting him who called you in the grace of Christ and are turning to a different gospel."

You got it, right? This isn't for nonbelievers. It's for *us*.

Paul continued, "Not that there is another one, but there are some who trouble you and want to distort the gospel of Christ. But even if we or an angel from heaven should preach to you a gospel contrary to the one we preached to you, let him be accursed. As we have said before, so now I say again: If anyone is preaching to you a gospel contrary to the one you received, let him be accursed" (vv. 7–9).

> **THERE'S NOTHING TOUCHY-FEELY ABOUT WHAT PAUL WAS SAYING TO THESE BELIEVERS.**

I told you it was rough. There's nothing touchy-feely about what Paul was saying to these believers.

In the same letter, Paul cried out, "O foolish Galatians! Who has bewitched you? It was before your eyes that Jesus Christ was publicly portrayed as crucified. Let me ask you only this: Did you receive the Spirit by the works of the law or by hearing with faith? Are you so foolish?" I want you to get this because Paul was just heartbroken. "Having begun by the Spirit, are you now being perfected by the flesh?" (3:1–3).

He was pointing them back to the beginning, that faith that began with the Spirit. He was waking them up!

When those young men and women I mentioned earlier at TVC finally responded to the gospel, they woke up. Way too many of us today are like the Galatians: We heard the gospel, we received the gospel, and then we got sleepy. I want you to hear God's voice, through Paul, that invites us to wake up—for the first time or for the first time in a long time—to the gospel of Jesus Christ.

REFLECT

1. As you consider your own story, is it more like the Galatians—who began with the Spirit and got bewitched—or is it more like some of the young adults I mentioned earlier, who may have been sleeping from the jump and then were woken up by the Spirit?

   _____
   _____
   _____
   _____
   _____
   _____

2. As you review Paul's words, which of them are speaking directly to *you* today?

   _____
   _____
   _____
   _____
   _____
   _____

CHALLENGE

Notice again Paul's words: "There are some who trouble you and want to distort the gospel of Christ" (Galatians 1:7). Do you see it? After we've received the true gospel, there are some who will distort it. We receive what is true, and then it becomes distorted. Today, I want you to notice and name the ways in which the pure gospel you received when you came to know Christ personally has been distorted. Honestly, that can come from outside of you—such as the teachings of others—and it can also come from inside of you, your temptation to add or remove what does or does not suit you. This is a good one to record in a journal because if you do it honestly, it can launch you into a new season with Christ.

DAY 10 SEEK ONLY JESUS

O foolish Galatians! Who has bewitched you? It was before your eyes that Jesus Christ was publicly portrayed as crucified. Let me ask you only this: Did you receive the Spirit by works of the law or by hearing with faith? Are you so foolish? Having begun by the Spirit, are you now being perfected by the flesh? Did you suffer so many things in vain—if indeed it was in vain? Does he who supplies the Spirit to you and works miracles among you do so by works of the law, or by hearing with faith?

GALATIANS 3:1–5

LET'S SAY YOU'RE a college student and you've had an encounter with Jesus. You decide to trust Him with your life, and you know Him *personally*. When you graduate, you count on Jesus to keep you safe when your hand-me-down car breaks down on the freeway. You're not making much money, but you trust Him to help you pay the rent every month. And you talk to Jesus daily about the coworker you think might be your potential spouse.

A few decades later, you're driving a shiny new Lexus. You're pulling some coin. You're married to that coworker, and you have three kids. But what's a little bit different is that you're pretty comfortable in a lot of ways. If you're honest, you don't *have* to trust Jesus for much of anything. You never meant to stop talking to Jesus daily, but things just happened. *Life* happened.

This was what was going on in the early church. Because in Galatia, the gospel had gone out: It was received, it took root, and it sprang up with great gladness. And then this group of people from Jerusalem called the Judaizers swung into Galatia. They began to teach that in order to be a Christian, you had to conform to the moral and dietary laws of the Old Testament: You had to be circumcised, you couldn't eat that pork sandwich anymore, and you had to put down that crispy bacon.

And people started to buy it. They began to believe that Jesus wasn't enough. They started to believe that it was Jesus *plus* the law. They began to be deceived. The word Paul used in Galatians 3:1 is translated as "bewitched." Like someone had put a spell on them. And Paul was baffled by it. He was confounded.

> **YOU WERE MADE FOR SO MUCH MORE BECAUSE YOU WERE MADE FOR SO MUCH LESS.**

SEEK ONLY JESUS | 55

"What happened to you?" He was trying to wake them up. He was reminding them of the goodness of Jesus. The sufficiency of Jesus. And I love what he did next. He asked them, "How did this thing get started?"

Now, here's what's awesome. I know how it happened for you. And for me. Because it happened for all of us in the same way. I want to highlight Romans 5:8: "But God shows his love for us in that while we were still sinners, Christ died for us." And again in Ephesians 1:3–6: "Blessed be the God and Father of our Lord Jesus Christ, who has blessed us in Christ with every spiritual blessing in the heavenly places, even as he chose us in him before the foundation of the world, that we should be holy and blameless before him. In love he predestined us for adoption to himself as sons through Jesus Christ, according to the purpose of his will, to the praise of his glorious grace, with which he has blessed us in the Beloved."

This is where we *all* start. At the beginning—for me, for you, for the believers in Ephesus—it was *just* Jesus.

When we look at Scripture, when we look around our churches, we can see folks who started with *just* Jesus. But then "just Jesus" becomes Jesus *plus* my 401(k). Or Jesus *plus* the rental property that pays for itself because we Airbnb it. Jesus *plus* the "perfect" family. Jesus *plus* the specialist at the world-renowned medical complex who is our family's last hope.

You were made for so much more because you were made for so much less. You don't need that *extra*. You were saved before the foundation of the earth was laid. The Lord said, "I'm gonna love him." "I'm gonna love her." *That's your story.* I know it sounds unsophisticated to say that you were born for *just* Jesus. But I'm still saying it. If you've been lulled into thinking that you need anything more than the person of Jesus, then you've been lied to.

You need Jesus. Plus *nothing*.

> **YOU NEED JESUS. PLUS *NOTHING*.**

REFLECT

1. Consider any drift that has happened in your walk with God, because there was a day when you needed only Jesus. What have you added to that in order to feel more comfortable or secure?

_____
_____
_____
_____
_____
_____

2. If you were to choose to return to "just Jesus," what would look different in your life?

_____
_____
_____
_____
_____
_____

CHALLENGE

If you've known financial instability, it's natural that you're going to be tempted to find security in having enough money to keep you comfortable. If you or someone you love has had a health scare, it's normal that you want to seek out the best medical care you can find. And there are certainly ways in which God can be at work in both. But you were made for Jesus plus nothing. So I'm inviting you today to create a list of the extras in your life that you depend on *in addition* to knowing Jesus. Don't worry, because I'm not going to ask you to empty your bank account or fire your doctor. What I want you to do is to be as thorough as possible, making a list of all your "pluses," and offer it to God. Leave it with God as a simple way to grow in your trust of Him.

DAY 11
RECEIVE NEW MERCIES

Remember my affliction and my wanderings, the wormwood and the gall! My soul continually remembers it and is bowed down within me. But this I call to mind, and therefore I have hope: The steadfast love of the Lord never ceases; his mercies never come to an end; they are new every morning; great is your faithfulness.

LAMENTATIONS 3:19–23

I HAVE FRIENDS who pastor in extremely secular cities like Seattle, Portland, and New York. Their environments and overall culture are far more hostile toward the church than what I experience in the suburbs of Dallas. These friends and I have often sat around a fire pit and discussed the difficulties of ministry in our contexts. After these conversations, I am usually persuaded that I have the tougher job in the Bible Belt.

C. S. Lewis, in his book *The Problem of Pain*, says, "Prostitutes are in no danger of finding their present life so satisfactory that they cannot turn to God: the proud, the avaricious, the self-righteous, are in that danger."[1] Lewis was pointing out a disposition Christians can develop if we aren't careful. The disposition tends to reveal itself by the speed at which we can point to the irreligious as those who need to be saved. Perhaps this is your story. It could be.

Maybe you got saved out of licentiousness. You acted like you were a better god than God. You told God that you didn't need Him by doing whatever you wanted to do. You were saved from the kind of license in which you just decided to do whatever you wanted. That might be you.

But I need to name, again, that it's also possible that you got saved out of church stuff. Out of legalism. You told God that you didn't need Him by your frantic religious activity. We know that it's a trap people can fall into. They go to a church and connect there, and they get involved, but they never actually have a love relationship with Jesus. Because you can put on the clothes, you can embrace the culture, and you can do the things that church values. You can figure it out. You can do all that and not have a deep love relationship with Jesus.

> **YOU'RE ACTING LIKE YOU'VE GOT TO *EARN* THIS THING THAT YOU WERE GIVEN. YOU. DO. NOT.**

RECEIVE NEW MERCIES | 61

But Paul wasn't having it. Paul was reminding the believers, "This is where you were when Jesus moved toward you and saved you. You were at your worst. Your sin—however it was expressed—didn't take Jesus by surprise. Jesus knew what He was buying on the cross. He knew exactly what you were. You did nothing to be saved. You only received. But something hoodwinked you, and now you're acting like you've got to *earn* this thing that you were given. You. Do. Not" (Romans 5:8, paraphrased).

> **GOD IS GOOD. HE MOVES TOWARD YOU.**

God is good. He moves toward you. He purchased you at your worst, not at your best. In fact, the spiritual life is this long journey home. It's two steps forward and one step back. But that's still one step forward. It's thinking we have the victory and realizing we don't. So we take it back to Jesus again. It's long-suffering. And so we continue to press in. We refuse to believe the lie of the Enemy. We receive God's new mercies every morning (Lamentations 3:22–23). We get back after it.

Beloved, God offers us a covenantal relationship that means, "I'm with you, no matter what" (Matthew 28:20, paraphrased). And then we try to trade that in for a contractual relationship. Christians are choked out of the glory of the gospel by this insidious lie. It's a misunderstanding of who God actually is. It's thin and weak and will not prevail. So God is saying, "Covenant, no matter what. You're weak. But I got this. You're my son. You're my daughter. I've got you. I'm your Father. As Ephesians 1:3 says, all the spiritual blessings in the heavenly places are yours."

And how do we respond? We're like, "How about I try to do better in these ways . . . ? And when I do better in these ways, I might be able to believe what is true about me, that I'm Yours."

I need you to hear God saying, "What the heck are you doing? I love you. I want to be in relationship with you."

And we're stubborn. So we're quick to say, "Okay, as long as I can base that on my effort. As long as Your offer is based on me trying to be better."

No. Just no.

Whether irreligiously or religiously, you were a train wreck when God saved you. But your salvation is not one-and-done. It doesn't depend on your performance. No, because when you blow it—which you will—God's mercies are new every morning. That means that when you blow it, you return to the One whose faithful covenant love does not fail.

REFLECT

1. What are some of the ways in which you're tempted to earn God's love or God's favor?

_____
_____
_____
_____
_____
_____

2. Are you in the habit of going to God and asking for His new mercies when you blow it? Why or why not?

_____
_____
_____
_____
_____
_____

CHALLENGE

Depending on the church tradition in which you were raised—or *not* raised—you might have been taught to pray a prayer of confession. In some churches that's a prayer printed in a bulletin; in others, it might be a silent moment when you have to get honest with God, confess your sins, and ask for forgiveness. What's good about this kind of prayer is that it is a way to live out the reality that God's mercies are new every morning. We get forgiven again and again. Today, take whatever cruddy sins have built up in your life since the last time you confessed them—which may have been yesterday or two decades ago. Offer your sins to God, and receive His fresh mercies today. And tomorrow. And the next day.

DAY 12 COMMIT TO MORAL HOLINESS

Therefore, preparing your minds for action, and being sober-minded, set your hope fully on the grace that will be brought to you at the revelation of Jesus Christ. As obedient children, do not be conformed to the passions of your former ignorance, but as he who called you is holy, you also be holy in all your conduct, since it is written, "You shall be holy, for I am holy."

1 PETER 1:13–16

WE ALL ENTER our relationship with Jesus with a backstory. Some of us are dragging along an addiction to porn or a habit of lying, while others have developed other unhealthy habits. The longer we put off surrendering to Jesus, the more complex our backstories can get. I knew an older man whose real estate business dealings were oppressive to those who were experiencing poverty. Think about having to unravel that.

I think we've established that we're all coming to God with some kind of a mess. And I am not going to pretend that when we say yes to Jesus, somehow the mess we brought magically disappears. Usually, it doesn't. The longing for the drug might remain. The hunger to binge is still there. We're still carrying around the temptation to have sex whenever we want with whomever we want.

It would be great if salvation was a magic wand that made that all disappear, but magic is not what God has promised us.

While those who are in a spiritual coma may ignore it, when we're in a relationship with Jesus, the Holy Spirit is going to grow us and increase our external moral holiness. Did you know that this is God's good intention in your life? Not just to bend down and put a gold cross lapel pin on you while you're in the gutter—signaling to whoever's guarding the pearly gates that you should be admitted—but to lift you up and stand you on solid ground. That's what being intimate with Jesus leads to. It leads to moral holiness. I know that wording might sound a little shady or suspect because our culture has tainted and stained it. Living a life of moral holiness means that God is setting you free for life that really is *life*.

> **LIVING A LIFE OF MORAL HOLINESS MEANS THAT GOD IS SETTING YOU FREE FOR LIFE THAT REALLY IS *LIFE*.**

> **GROWING IN MORAL HOLINESS ISN'T LIKELY GOING TO SHOW UP AS A VIRAL TIKTOK VIDEO.**

Growing in moral holiness isn't likely going to show up as a viral TikTok video. It's not going to become the new fad on college campuses. It may not even be very popular at your church! But when we come to know Him, God invites each one of us to become more holy. And that means, with God, we put our sins to death.

The way to do that is to be serious about sin. Yes, have some discipline. But I want to make sure you know how it works. The big win is that one kind of wickedness, one affection that's robbing you of life, is actually driven out by a greater affection. Does that make sense? You lose affection for *this thing* when the affection for *the other* overpowers it. Not when you just decide, *I'm done with porn forever.* Or weed. Or the bottle. Or the other sinful habit or addiction. A greater affection, a genuine affection for God that is rooted in a relationship with Christ, drives out lesser affections.

You get how that's good news, right?

When the greater affection drives out those lesser affections, you experience the light and life of becoming awake—whether you've never had a relationship with Jesus or you're waking back up to the goodness of a personal relationship with Jesus.

If Jesus is waking you up in these pages, by the power of His Word, I want you to get really honest about the lesser affections you've allowed to remain in your life. Whether you've been walking with Jesus for five days or five decades, I want you to look at your life and ask for the Spirit to show you which affections need to go.

It may be an addiction to social media or bingeing streaming shows.

It may be spending your money on that which has no kingdom value.

Maybe it's the fixation on your appearance that you know does not honor God.

Ask the Spirit to bring to mind the choices you're making that God wants to transform.

And *how* do we kick these lesser affections? A lot of times we behave as if what we have to do is try really hard. Or *finally* be disciplined. But I'm suggesting that you flip it. Rather than cutting out the death-dealing thing, fill yourself with the life-giving thing. Only light can drive out darkness. And growing in your affection for Jesus is what will drive out the lesser affections that are afflicting you.

REFLECT

1. Over the course of your relationship with Christ, in what ways have you grown in moral holiness?

___

2. In what areas have you failed to become morally holy as you've walked with Jesus?

___

CHALLENGE

Today's challenge is a little counterintuitive. Because whenever we're trying to tackle a sin, to kill the flesh, we naturally try to exercise fortitude. Discipline. Willpower. Sometimes it works. Other times it does not. But today, instead of telling you to buckle down to tackle whatever lesser affections have gripped you, I'm challenging you to invest in your "first love": your affection for God (Revelation 2:4). You're trusting that the greater affection will drive out the lesser one. When we set our hope, our minds, our hearts, our time, and our energy on Christ, we are pursuing holiness. Decide today what specific action steps you'll take in order to increase your intimacy with and affection for Christ.

DAY 13 STOP SINNING

Everyone who makes a practice of sinning also practices lawlessness; sin is lawlessness. You know that he appeared in order to take away sins, and in him there is no sin. No one who abides in him keeps on sinning; no one who keeps on sinning has either seen him or known him. Little children, let no one deceive you. Whoever practices righteousness is righteous, as he is righteous. Whoever makes a practice of sinning is of the devil, for the devil has been sinning from the beginning. The reason the Son of God appeared was to destroy the works of the devil.

1 JOHN 3:4–8

YOU MAY NOT be a Christian.

Did I get your attention? I hope so. Because the way that we navigate sin—whether we're refusing to acknowledge it or whether we're going after it head-on—actually determines whether or not we can call ourselves "Christian."

So let's talk about sin. My sin doesn't look like your sin. Yours doesn't look like mine or the next guy's. But what I know for sure is that we both have it. So let's not dodge it. Let's talk about it.

LET'S NOT DODGE IT. LET'S TALK ABOUT IT.

Some people like to say that all we need to do is believe in Jesus and we'll be saved. We do need to believe in Jesus. But it's not just belief. I'll be careful but direct here: It's also *growing in external holiness*.

A question highlighting a biblical principle in Romans 6:1 asks, "Are we to continue in sin that grace may abound?" To be clear, it's rhetorical. The answer is no.

Let's say you were a friend of mine, and you kept sinning. I'd gently say something to you, I'd name the sin, because I love you. I'd want to say what John was saying in 1 John 3: "You're not a Christian, man. I'm sorry. I know you got baptized when you were six. You consider yourself a good person. You just practice sinning all the time."

I want to be clear about this: I'm not talking about *stumbling*. We all stumble. First John 1:8 says, "If we say we have no sin, we deceive ourselves, and the truth is not in us." So I'm not saying we don't stumble. You do. I do.

I'm addressing something different. You've been baptized, you're in church, and you're a generally moral person, but your life is marked by a practice of sin and ongoing unrighteousness that you're not willing to put to death. This is what I want to deal with. There's just not a world that allows me to say, "You can do that and be a Christian. You can make that sinful choice and call yourself a Christian." There's nothing in the Bible, or throughout Christian history, that makes room for this category where you can do whatever you want, but as long as you believe that Jesus was the Son of God, it's all good. It's just not there.

You already know I'm not talking about stumbling. No, it's this: *You need to hate sin.* You need to be serious about putting it to death. (And, man, it's a fight.) If this is where you are, if you need to get serious about putting sin to death, brother or sister, you are in good company. There are folks all around you on a Sunday morning who are in the same boat.

I'm making it plain here: If you plunge headlong into sin, if you're walking in wickedness, you cannot consider yourself a Christian. There's no fruit that you are. Belief is not enough because we need both belief *and* an ongoing shaping to external moral holiness according to God's commands in the Scriptures.

It's messy.

It's slow.

There will be stumbling.

Feel familiar?

Jesus says we should make disciples of all nations, "teaching them to observe all that I have commanded" (Matthew 28:19–20). He didn't say "teaching them to *know* all I have commanded." It's teaching them to *obey*.

I am so serious about this stuff, and my congregation knows it. In fact, at the end of the service, when we might dim the lights, close our eyes, bow our heads, and pray—we *don't*. That's not a private moment anymore in our church. And the reason is that we don't want individuals to be left alone, believing that they're the only ones who struggle. Or are asleep. No, we want to be bold about it. So I ask people to keep every eye open, every head up, and turn up the lights as bright as they can get in the room. Believe me, there's no shame. We're not about that shame game. No, we're about being a body who hates sin and wants to be transformed to look more like Jesus.

> **WE DON'T WANT INDIVIDUALS TO BE LEFT ALONE, BELIEVING THAT THEY'RE THE ONLY ONES WHO STRUGGLE.**

Sister or brother, if you're stuck in some chronic sin, I'm giving you the opportunity to see it. To name it. And to reject it. And I need you to know that it's possible. You can reject sin with the help of Jesus Christ and begin to bear fruit.

REFLECT

1. What's the sticky sin in your life? What's the one that's been hard to overcome?

_____
_____
_____
_____
_____
_____
_____

2. In what ways have you *tried* to shake this sin?

_____
_____
_____
_____
_____
_____
_____

CHALLENGE

I need you to know that you are not alone. I understand how scary it can feel to release the sin that is so familiar and comfortable that we'd rather keep it than kick it to the curb. But if your life is marked by a practice of sin and ongoing unrighteousness, I am certain that God can set you free from it. So I want you to ask the Spirit to help you identify the one sin that God wants to help you overcome today. (It may be a different one tomorrow!) Identify the sin that, *today*, God is inviting you to put to death. Today, tomorrow, and the next day, keep offering that sin to God and asking Him to help you release it forever. You've got this.

DAY 14: LOVE THE FAMILY OF FAITH

For this is the message that you have heard from the beginning, that we should love one another. We should not be like Cain, who was of the evil one and murdered his brother. And why did he murder him? Because his own deeds were evil and his brother's righteous. Do not be surprised, brothers, that the world hates you. We know that we have passed out of death into life, because we love the brothers. Whoever does not love abides in death.

1 JOHN 3:11–14

MAYBE YOU'VE SEEN some of the same folks that I have who call themselves Christians. They like to be out on the street where they can be seen and heard by all. They carry big signs, conveniently designed so that those in cars driving by—or flying in rockets in space—can read them. These big-letter signs might have any number of exclamation points following some kind of accusation or judgment against some group of people or another. They often carry megaphones, but they must not trust these instruments to do their jobs because they *shout* into the megaphones. They're projecting a lot of volume. They're slamming down judgment. They're carrying a lot of conviction that they're right.

What they're missing is *love*.

I'll bet you're familiar with this stereotype—based on real events—of the Holy Roller Christian who's overly concerned about the behavior of others. This is the brother or sister who always has something unkind to say—in the name of Jesus. Truly, they may really believe that by pointing out the failures of others, they're doing their jobs.

Jesus never gave them that job.

I know this because it's in *the Bible*. The Word says that one of the ways you know you've believed the gospel of Jesus—that your submission to Jesus is real—is that you love the brothers. You love the sisters. Actually, the elders in the early church had a word for the men and women of God: They called all the brothers and sisters alike *the brethren*. First John 3:14 announces,

> **OUR LOVE FOR OUR BROTHERS AND SISTERS IS THE EVIDENCE THAT WE'VE BEEN SAVED.**

LOVE THE FAMILY OF FAITH | 79

"We know that we have passed out of death and into life, because we love the brothers. Whoever does not love abides in death." This verse is saying that our love for our brothers and sisters is the evidence that we've been saved.

This is big, right? It is. But it's not saying you have to *like* all of us. And I'm going to suggest that the way you can love someone, even when you don't necessarily like them, is to understand that we're all caught up in the same story. There might be something about you that bothers me a little bit. There's *certainly* something about me that bothers you a little bit. Yet we have this shared experience, this shared story, so I love you.

It doesn't always look like this, does it? We're not always feeling or offering the love.

You and I can both agree that those who do nothing but accuse the brethren are of Satan and not of Christ. (I know I just got myself in trouble. I stand by it.) This message is woven throughout the Scriptures.

These are folks who see it as their job, their fixation, to police the brethren. To critique the brethren. And hammer the brethren by pointing out our failures.

Is there a place for gently helping a brother or sister recognize and conquer some besetting sin in their life? Galatians 6:1 says there is. With wisdom and prayer, we are to help our siblings in the family of faith to live well. Should we be wise and discerning like that? Absolutely. But should we have a critical spirit that weighs in on everybody else while minimizing our own sin? If you do, if that's the default position you have toward the brethren, I think you're either sound asleep or not a believer. Scripture is clear.

A love for the brethren is what marks those who are genuinely alive in Christ. If you've never heard that before, hear it now. In fact, I suspect it's something you've probably known in your gut. Because we notice these folks around us who are filled with love for others, right? We see it in the way they treat others. In the way they speak to them. And we can even see it in the faces and eyes of those who *love well*.

I'm wondering who you've noticed loving others really, really well. It might be the older woman who offers a room in her home to the young woman who needs to leave sin behind but hasn't been able to do it financially. Or it could be as simple as the college-age young man or woman who agrees to join a friend's sobriety support group, even though he or she doesn't wrestle with abusing alcohol. I'm confident that as we submit ourselves to Christ, He will become our coach as we devote ourselves to living a life of love among the ones He loves.

> **A LOVE FOR THE BRETHREN IS WHAT MARKS THOSE WHO ARE GENUINELY ALIVE IN CHRIST.**

REFLECT

1. Rather than pointing the finger of judgment at others who point the finger of judgment, consider the areas in your life where you struggle to love others well. In what relationships do you face the biggest challenges?

_____

_____

_____

_____

_____

2. In what areas are you succeeding at loving those whom others might struggle to embrace and love well?

_____

_____

_____

_____

_____

CHALLENGE

Today's challenge is going to be unique to you. That means I want you to search your heart and notice where it's particularly difficult for you to love someone—or several someones—well. For instance, you might be the megaphone holder who struggles to love the "sinners" you're railing against. Or you may struggle *more* with finding any love in your heart at all for the person holding the megaphone. (It just got real, didn't it?) Let God's Spirit show you who He is calling you to love well. And then, today, take your first step in practicing love for the "other" God is showing you.

DAY 15 BELIEVE IN THE MIRACULOUS

Now you are the body of Christ and individually members of it. And God has appointed in the church first apostles, second prophets, third teachers, then miracles, then gifts of healing, helping, administrating, and various kinds of tongues. Are all apostles? Are all prophets? Are all teachers? Do all work miracles? Do all possess gifts of healing? Do all speak with tongues? Do all interpret? But earnestly desire the higher gifts.

1 CORINTHIANS 12:27–31

IN THE LATE fall and winter of 1819–1820, a seventy-seven-year-old Thomas Jefferson bought a Bible and a razor blade.[1] And then over a period of time he sat with the Bible, blade in hand, and worked his way through the four Gospels. He went line by line through Matthew,

Mark, Luke, and John and cut out any reference to the miraculous, any reference to the deity of Christ, and anything other than the moral teachings of Jesus. Then he published it under the title *The Life and Morals of Jesus of Nazareth*. Today it's called the Jefferson Bible. In Washington, DC, you can find a copy of it in the Smithsonian and also at the Museum of the Bible.

> **HE THOUGHT MIRACLES WERE HOGWASH.**

So let's look at what was happening in 1819. It was almost the apex of the Enlightenment, an era in which people believed there was a natural, reasonable explanation for anything. So you can see how that had shaped Jefferson. What he recognized in the person of Jesus, what a lot of people see in Jesus, was some wisdom for life, some morality. Jefferson's big idea was that if we would listen to Jesus' moral teachings and live our lives in alignment with these principles, good things would happen for a town, a city, a nation. Thomas Jefferson believed *that*, but he didn't believe in the deity of Christ. He thought miracles were hogwash. And so he offered the world the Jefferson Bible.[2]

It's powerful, isn't it? It's such a vivid representation of taking what we like from the Bible and rejecting what we don't. I suspect we're all tempted to do it. But Jefferson was really bold about it.

Now, you and I, in the time that God placed us, are going to repeatedly find ourselves smashing against this kind of thinking. And I find it sad that so many Christians today would likely testify with their mouths that they believe in miracles—when they read from

BELIEVE IN THE MIRACULOUS | 85

the creeds of the church that affirm a virgin gave birth to the Son of God—but then live as if none of it is available to them.

Today there's a mindset in the West that the world is not enchanted—that there's nothing supernatural at play. Just give us enough time, and we'll find the explanation for it through natural means. But if I got on a plane and flew to India tomorrow, I wouldn't find this mindset there. Not in Africa. Not in Asia. They believe in an enchanted supernatural world where there's a god or something behind everything.

The more we fight against the pull to find natural explanations for spiritual realities—and admit that we really *are* weird, enchanted, supernatural people involved in a weird, enchanted, supernatural world—the more we take a step toward what God has for us to walk in. Acknowledging that the spiritual world exists is actually more normal than a lot of the nonsense we believe or embrace.

> **WE REALLY *ARE* WEIRD, ENCHANTED, SUPERNATURAL PEOPLE INVOLVED IN A WEIRD, ENCHANTED, SUPERNATURAL WORLD.**

That's what Paul was getting after in the letter he wrote to the church in Corinth about spiritual giftings. It's why it's important for us to understand the enchanted world we're in. As believers, we hold fast to there being something more than what we can hear and smell and touch and taste and see.

First Corinthians 12:27–31

is just one passage in which Paul was trying to communicate, "Hey, there's more available to you." If you know it in your head, are you living it? Or have you been living from that razor-cut Bible? When Paul said earlier in this chapter that "to each is given the manifestation of the Spirit for the common good" (v. 7), that includes you. You have been given the Spirit. He is real, and you were created to move as an agent of God in this enchanted world.

It can be tempting for a lot of Christians to believe that God has given spiritual gifts to other folks (and we're okay with that), but that He hasn't given them a particular gift. Yet Paul was reminding the church that God gave *each one* a manifestation of the Spirit for the common good. That means me. And you. And Uncle Ernie. And the woman who lives in the house on the corner. And if you read through that list of gifts, you'll see the ways in which they are absolutely given for the good of others.

Learn from Jefferson's foolishness. Embrace the spiritual gift God has given you, and use it for the good of others.

REFLECT

1. Get honest, and then privately, quietly, with God, list the parts of the Bible that you would cut out. Why did you choose those?

_____

_____

_____

_____

_____

_____

_____

2. What spiritual gifts has God placed in you to be used for the good of others?

_____

_____

_____

_____

_____

_____

_____

CHALLENGE

Your challenge today is to be intentional about embracing the enchanted world. (No, that's not Narnia, the Shire, or Hogwarts. Stay with me here.) What will it look like for you to choose to acknowledge a spiritual reality that is more real than what we can see with our eyes? I'm going to guess that you know a Christian who is keenly aware of the way the spiritual world intersects with the world around us. Sometime in the next week or two, invite that person to coffee—your treat—and ask them to share how they've experienced the reality of the spiritual world. Then ask God how He wants you to apply what you've discovered.

DAY 16: MATURE BY SERVING

To each is given the manifestation of the Spirit for the common good. For to one is given through the Spirit the utterance of wisdom, and to another the utterance of knowledge according to the same Spirit, to another faith by the same Spirit, to another gifts of healing by the one Spirit, to another the working of miracles, to another prophecy, to another the ability to distinguish between spirits, to another various kinds of tongues, to another the interpretation of tongues. All these are empowered by one and the same Spirit, who apportions to each one individually as he wills.

1 CORINTHIANS 12:7–11

A FEW MONTHS ago, I flew to Boise, Idaho. It sounds beautiful, doesn't it? I was speaking at a conference where we were talking about the future of the church. The organizers had asked me to explain The Village Church's model of doing church and the pros and cons of that. One of the primary cons that I candidly shared with this group was that for whatever beautiful, good, amazing things God has done at The Village Church during the last twenty years, we have still been unable to dismantle the consumeristic mentality of the suburbs. What I mean by that is that many, many people in our congregation still think that all the volunteers who show up week after week exist only to serve them. And they fail to see spiritual formation as something that Jesus requires from them. They refuse to see that they're called to sacrifice in order to serve others. Lots of incredible things have happened in our congregation, but this has been one nut we've had a hard time cracking.

> **YOU WILL GROW IN GLADNESS WHEN YOU UNDERSTAND ALL THE GIFTS OF YOUR LIFE HAVE BEEN GIVEN TO YOU FOR OTHERS' SAKE.**

In 1 Corinthians 12:7–11, the apostle Paul was saying "No, no, no" to each one of these shirkers. There's been given a manifestation of the Spirit, something of the Spirit, not for you alone but for the common good. This means the church will never be fully "we" until you deposit into your local church community the good gifts that God put in you for our sake. And our church, just like so many others, is consistently running and driven by this 15 to 20 percent of people who are serving everywhere.

MATURE BY SERVING | 91

The rebuke from this text should be to you: You will not mature in Christ as long as you see your maturation as just about you, the Bible, and some prayer time. No, you will grow spiritually when you give yourself to others over and over and over again. And you will grow in gladness when you understand all the gifts of your life have been given to you for others' sake and not for your sake—for the glory of God and the church's good as a community. And so I had to be honest that in twenty years we haven't been able to dismantle the thing.

Believe me, I speak honestly about it to our congregation in worship service. I'll be intentional, in a playful way, rebuking folks. They'll agree for a minute, and then we're back to business as usual. I confess to them, "I just don't know what to do." The latent potential in our own body of believers drives me nuts. I love these folks, but we've got some sleeping, sleepy, lazy, "sit on our hands and watch other people serve the kingdom" folks. Every church does.

> **I KNOW WE'RE MADE FOR SO MUCH MORE.**

It keeps me up at night because I know we're made for so much more. We're made to be a body in which every member is serving and growing. And without serving, there isn't growth. There isn't maturation. There isn't transformation. I want to holler, "Good God! What are you doing? You're not going to mature in gladness and zeal for the Lord as long as you think everybody else exists to rub your shoulders into maturity. Nope, that's not how it works." No, the Word says, "To each is given the manifestation of the Spirit for the common good" (v. 7).

Because you were designed by God to serve, we need the gifts that *only you* can bring. If you've been given a gift, which you have, and you're not serving, then we're all in trouble. It's bad for the body and it's bad for you, because you mature by serving. You mature by dying to yourself. You don't mature by allowing others to serve you until you get mature. That's not how it works. The body of Christ needs what only you can bring.

It might be the utterance of wisdom. Or knowledge. It might be your gift of faith. It may be the gift of healing that we can't do without. Or the working of miracles. Or announcing prophecy. And as everyone explodes into using their gifts, we're definitely going to need you if you have the ability to distinguish between spirits. We need the person gifted with speaking in tongues to be speaking; we need the one gifted to interpret those words to do their job too. We need it all.

Today, are you in that 80 to 85 percent of Christians who are coasting? Are you sitting back and letting the weary warriors at your church do all the heavy lifting? While it sounds like some sort of privilege to sit back like that, it's not. It's not a privilege because it keeps you from growing. It keeps you from maturing.

Sister or brother, this one keeps me up at night. I so want to see every Christian growing more and more into the image of Jesus, and that only happens when each one is serving with the gifts they've been given.

REFLECT

1. In this demonstrated metric[1] that 15 to 20 percent of folks in churches are doing the lion's share of the work of serving, where do you land? Why?

   _____
   _____
   _____
   _____
   _____

2. If your church purposed to look more like a church where 100 percent of the congregation shared the work of serving, how would you need to change? Would you need to step up or step back?

   _____
   _____
   _____
   _____
   _____

CHALLENGE

I hope you understand clearly what I'm saying with this invitation to serve. I'm not saying that because we need more accountants to balance our books to keep our organization running. Not at all. I'm saying that for God's kingdom to reign on earth as it does in heaven (Matthew 6:10), we need you to bring the gifts that only you can bring. For you to be fully awake and alive in Christ, you need to be serving. In today's Scripture passage and yesterday's, both from 1 Corinthians 12, what are the gifts God has given you and called you to use? With that in mind, what's your *next* step?

DAY 17
PRAY BIG

Is anyone among you suffering? Let him pray. Is anyone cheerful? Let him sing praise. Is anyone among you sick? Let him call for the elders of the church, and let them pray over him, anointing him with oil in the name of the Lord. And the prayer of faith will save the one who is sick, and the Lord will raise him up. And if he has committed sins, he will be forgiven. Therefore, confess your sins to one another and pray for one another, that you may be healed. The prayer of a righteous person has great power as it is working.

JAMES 5:13–16

THERE'S A WOMAN in our congregation whom I'll call Liv. After Liv was diagnosed with esophageal cancer, we prayed for her, thanking God for His common-grace gift of chemotherapy and radiation. And when those good gifts of God worked, we thanked and praised Him.

But as she was recovering, Liv noticed that her back was killing her. She was enduring excruciating pain across her lower back, from side to side. On a scale of 1 to 10, it was level 9 pain. It was brutal. An MRI showed that her spine was covered in cancer and her vertebrae had been crushed. At that point they put her on palliative care for comfort. They'd give her as much pain medicine as she wanted to keep her comfortable. They told her to gather her family to share the news that she'd been given nine to twelve months to live. It was time to get her house in order.

The doctors prescribed chemo and radiation again, and they wanted to do a PET scan to see the extent of the cancer. It was scheduled ten days after Liv received the diagnosis.

Liv's husband, Dave, was keeping up a CaringBridge page, letting friends and family know how she was doing and asking them to pray. On the morning of the PET scan, the Lord prompted Dave to ask everyone to pray for Liv's healing that day.

And they did.

She had the PET scan, and that evening, just as the couple was walking into their home, the phone rang. The doctor was calling to let them know that the PET scan was clear.

Liv didn't need chemo.

Liv didn't need radiation.

Liv didn't have cancer.

The doctors were baffled, right? Of course they were. Just to rule it

> **THE AFTERNOON OF THE PET SCAN, HE WENT AHEAD AND TOLD EVERYONE SHE'D BEEN HEALED.**

out, they wanted to do a biopsy. Of course. Why not? They scheduled the biopsy for two weeks later.

I had to know what those two weeks were like for them. I mean, what was that wait like? How did they manage it? How did they walk that path? Well, I'll tell you what Dave did. The afternoon of the PET scan, he went ahead and told everyone she'd been healed.

Dave explained, "If the biopsy came back with cancer, I knew I was going to look pretty foolish." (He wasn't wrong.) But then Dave continued, "I didn't care. I'll be a fool for God."

Two weeks later, the biopsy came back completely clean.

Per the doctor's instructions, Liv and Dave had already prepared their family for the worst, for palliative care and no hope at all. Then . . . a miraculous healing.

> **I'M ASKING GOD TO GIVE ME MORE FAITH THAN I HAVE.**

During my last twenty years of ministry, there have been explicit miracles that simply have no explanation. I've seen maybe two or three dozen of them. And I've done hundreds of funerals.

What do we even make of this?

My prayer to God is, "Help me to believe more than I do right now." I'm asking God to give me more faith than I have.

But I'm not going to pretend like that's my own prayer. It's not. It's the prayer recorded in Mark 9:24 of a father whose son was getting beat up by something that had the kid in its grips. This dad did not know where to turn. No physician had been able to help him. There was no Mayo Clinic. But this father had *enough* faith to go to Jesus, right? That was a good first move. And when Jesus told this father, "All things are possible for one who believes" (v. 23), he wasn't going to risk it. So he cried out, "I believe; help my unbelief!" (v. 24). That's a solid prayer. And it was enough for Jesus.

Liv's husband, Dave, had enough faith to pray big from the jump. I might not have as much faith, so I ask God, "Help my unbelief."

REFLECT

1. What do you make of Dave's faith in what God could do? Do you know anyone like this who has giant, great big faith in what God can do when we ask? What was the last prayer you prayed that was full of giant, great big faith?

_____

_____

_____

_____

_____

2. Are you willing to ask God for more faith? Are you willing to offer whatever amount of faith you have right now and ask Him to give you more? Why or why not?

_____

_____

_____

_____

_____

CHALLENGE

You don't have to wait for a devastating diagnosis to start praying big. In fact, I don't advise it. I'm encouraging you to pray big right now. Maybe you have a child who's chosen not to walk with the Lord. Pray, "I believe; help my unbelief." Or maybe God has asked you to do something, and you've been pushing the Mute button on His voice. You've delayed your obedience because you're not sure you can do it. Pray, "I believe; help my unbelief." Choose one thing you're facing in your life today, and begin to *pray big*.

DAY 18
INCREASE YOUR FAITH

Do not be deceived, my beloved brothers. Every good gift and every perfect gift is from above, coming down from the Father of lights, with whom there is no variation or shadow due to change. Of his own will he brought us forth by the word of truth, that we should be a kind of firstfruits of his creatures.

JAMES 1:16–18

ROBERT, A HUSBAND and father of two married young adults, was incredibly active as a runner until he was diagnosed, at age sixty-two, with an aggressive, incurable brain tumor. He was a man of deep faith, committed to the work of the church. He and his wife served in children's ministry for decades, making a real impact in kids' lives.

When Robert got sick, the first thing his friends did was gather at the church to pray. The invitation went out far and wide, and several hundred people showed up to pray for Robert. These men loved Robert, and they knew no other place to go for help than to Jesus.

On this night when many gathered to pray, a lot of the prayers were cautious ones. They were noncommittal. No one would accuse anyone in this group of being too bold.

"God, we trust You, whatever may come."

"You got this, Lord. Do Your thing."

"If You want to heal him, go ahead. If not, we totally understand."

I'm not interested in judging people's prayers, but I think it's fair to say that these were not prayers that were full of faith.

Faith is the ability to trust God to accomplish what needs to be done. And it's different from saving faith; it's different from having faith in the finished work of Jesus to save you. That's not what this is about. No, this is a gift given to people who have seen God, gazed upon God, studied His Word, and seen His promises.

If you know any of these folks, they can seem overly optimistic. Annoyingly optimistic. It doesn't matter what happens; all they see is an opportunity for God to show off. Someone's just gotten the most awful diagnosis, and they're like, "Whoa, God, You've got to show Your face on this one." They just don't seem to be moved by any kind of brokenness or negativity. They only see opportunities for God to show up. That's the gift of faith:

> **THIS IS A GIFT GIVEN TO PEOPLE WHO HAVE SEEN GOD, GAZED UPON GOD, STUDIED HIS WORD, AND SEEN HIS PROMISES.**

INCREASE YOUR FAITH | 103

"Just come with me. He's got it. He's the King of the universe. He's the sovereign God. What can't He do? What is too hard for Him?" This is their faith.

No one has ever accused me of possessing this type of faith. I'm skeptical by nature, which makes me dig in and want to understand things clearly. It doesn't mean I don't have faith in what God can do, though, right? What it looks like is that when we're praying for the sick in a group, we'll begin by taking a few minutes to confess our doubts. Then I'll say, "Hey, God, I've got some doubts here. Right now. Increase my faith." After the confessions, we pray for the sick person.

We ask God to increase our faith. It's a gift that the Lord loves to give. It's one He wants us to ask for too. He wants us to beg for it. I continue to ask God to increase my faith because I want to be one of those people who are annoyingly optimistic. Amen?

> I CONTINUE TO ASK GOD TO INCREASE MY FAITH BECAUSE I WANT TO BE ONE OF THOSE PEOPLE WHO ARE ANNOYINGLY OPTIMISTIC.

James 1:17 tells us, "Every good gift and every perfect gift is from above, coming down from the Father of lights." But maybe you thought a "good gift" was a new Porsche or boat. Those aren't the kinds of gifts James was talking about. In fact, James had been writing about the testing of our faith. He actually believed that the testing of our faith is what produces steadfastness in us. (I'm not making this stuff up.) He said, "If any of you lacks wisdom, let him ask God" (1:5). When you read the first chapter of James's letter to the church, you're going to see that he considered "wisdom" to be a good gift. (The Porsche and the boat? Not so much for James.) And I'll say that faith is also one of the good gifts that God loves to give when we ask.

Friend, ask God to increase your faith. Go on and beg for it. That's a prayer that has legs. That's a prayer you can pray with confidence. Get after it.

REFLECT

1. When have you seen or known someone with the gift of faith? How did that person express that gift in the body of Christ?

_____
_____
_____
_____
_____

2. On a scale of 1 to 10, where would you say you land in terms of having the kind of faith that believes God can and will do what only God can and will do? (Hint: There's no shame here. We're all wired differently.)

_____
_____
_____
_____
_____

CHALLENGE

Today's challenge is very doable. Today, you're going to ask God for more faith. This is the faith of the father who brought his kid to Jesus in Mark 9. The boy was being bullied to death by a spirit, and this dad believed that Jesus could do something about it. I don't know if that dad showed up that day with a faith that would measure a 2, or if he was naturally more of a 9 guy. When Jesus announced that all things are possible for one who believes, this dad cried out, "I believe; help my unbelief!" (v. 24). That's the prayer. "I have faith; help me by giving me more faith." Make it your own.

DAY 19
ASK FOR GOD'S HELP

Shadrach, Meshach, and Abednego answered and said to the king, "O Nebuchadnezzar, we have no need to answer you in this matter. If this be so, our God whom we serve is able to deliver us from the burning fiery furnace, and he will deliver us out of your hand, O king. But if not, be it known to you, O king, that we will not serve your gods or worship the golden image that you have set up."

DANIEL 3:16–18

I WAS THIRTY-SIX years old—married and the father of three kids—when I was diagnosed with terminal brain cancer and given two to three years to live.

So picture me in the sanctuary of our church, and this group of people had gathered around me to pray. Afterward, a young man sat down next to me, gave me a hug, and asked, "Is God going to heal you?"

"Man," I answered, "I sure hope so."

Then he started crying. As I spoke with him a bit more, I found out why.

His uncle had told him that if I didn't believe that God would heal me outright, if I didn't have that faith, then I would die.

If anyone ever says that to you, they are a liar and a fool. You should run.

Now, to be fair, I was also experiencing the other side of that coin.

Have you ever been prayed for by somebody, when you're sick or in a lot of trouble, and they're reverent enough but they're also defending God just in case He doesn't come through? They're going to pray quietly because, if God doesn't show up, they don't want to look like a fool. They don't want God to look like He lacks power, right? Their prayers are trying to protect God as if He's a fragile thing.

Both of these approaches are not only wrong but also harmful.

I want to show you the way to pray.

In Daniel 3, Shadrach, Meshach, and Abednego were about to be thrown into the fiery furnace by King Nebuchadnezzar for not worshiping the golden idol. They said, "If this be so our God whom we serve is able to deliver us from the burning fiery furnace, and he will deliver us out of your hand, O king. But if not, be it known to you, O king, that we will not serve your gods or worship the golden image that you have set up" (vv. 17–18).

Boom.

Did you get that? "God is able. He can do it." That was their primary posture before God.

Their next posture is the one that

GOD IS ABLE.

many evangelicals have had a field day with: "God *will* do it." We say, "He will heal me; I'm believing by faith; He will heal me."

Now look again at these boys with the fire, at their third posture before God: "But even if He doesn't, He's God. I'm not. He's eternal. I'm not."

He can heal me. He will heal me. And even if He doesn't, He's God. My life is His.

That's the right posture before a God who heals and does miracles. If you miss any one of those three, then I think you've set yourself up to get angry at God for not doing something that He never promised you He would do.

I want to refer back to that dad who was full of faith in Mark 9. He said to Jesus, "I believe; help my unbelief!" (v. 24). You see the wisdom there?

Today, are you this desperate for God to come through in a way that only God can come through?

You've already received the bad news.

There are no other options.

There's no plan.

There's an addiction you haven't been able to shake.

There's some emotional trauma and brokenness that hasn't been able to be righted.

There's an illness, and you've lost hope.

And this sentence, given to us by the Holy Spirit, is actually the right posture: "I believe; help my unbelief!"

REFLECT

1. I was told that if I didn't have enough faith, I'd die. What other toxic spiritual messages have you heard when it comes to these brutal seasons of life?

   _____
   _____
   _____
   _____
   _____
   _____

2. As you think back to the kinds of conversations you've had with God, how have you been praying in these crisis situations? Which of the three postures have you assumed?

   _____
   _____
   _____
   _____
   _____
   _____

ASK FOR GOD'S HELP

CHALLENGE

Today's challenge is one I want you to lock in, pack up, and carry with you on the rest of your journey. Specifically, I want you to assume and practice the threefold posture of the three friends in a fiery furnace.

1. **GOD IS ABLE.** Read out loud passages from Scripture that proclaim God's power. For example, "Glory to God, who is able to do far beyond all that we could ask or imagine by his power at work within us" (Ephesians 3:20 CEB). Then pray it in your own words.

2. **HE WILL DO IT.** Read out loud Scripture verses that announce God's kindness, God's goodness, God's mercy, and God's willingness to intervene. For example, "But when the goodness and loving kindness of God our Savior appeared, he saved us, not because of works done by us in righteousness, but according to his own mercy" (Titus 3:4–5). Then pray it in your own words. If you're looking for more examples from the Bible, I love Romans 8:1, 31–39 as well as Ephesians 2:6–7.

3. **EVEN IF NOT, HE IS GOD.** Read out loud Scripture verses that celebrate God as the Master and Lord of all things. For example, "Worthy are you, our Lord and God, to receive glory and honor and power, for you created all things, and by your will they existed and were created" (Revelation 4:11). If you're wanting more Scripture here, Matthew 10:29–31 and Colossians 1:16–17 are helpful. Then pray it in your own words.

Continue to pray in this way, assuming this powerful threefold posture before God.

DAY 20: TRANSFORM CULTURE

So here's what I want you to do, God helping you: Take your everyday, ordinary life—your sleeping, eating, going-to-work, and walking-around life—and place it before God as an offering. Embracing what God does for you is the best thing you can do for him. Don't become so well-adjusted to your culture that you fit into it without even thinking. Instead, fix your attention on God. You'll be changed from the inside out. Readily recognize what he wants from you, and quickly respond to it.

ROMANS 12:1–2 MSG

I HAVE A confession to make: During the last two decades I've been pastoring, I've had a single-minded obsession. I have been captivated by the biblical, historical reality that the Holy Spirit can fall on a group of people in such a way as to transform a culture, drive out darkness, and establish light. If you don't believe me, then read the Bible. As I mentioned on Day 1, this actually happened in a city called Ephesus! That reality has rocked me, and it makes me hungry. It makes me pray.

In Ephesus, the Holy Spirit fell in such a way that the entire socioeconomic system turned on its head. What that means is that people who were making money from sinful gain gave it up. They repented and turned their backs on that wickedness. So today, you could imagine the raunchiest neighborhood where there are suddenly no strip clubs. There's no illicit drug use. There's a pervasive righteousness that settles over the entire city. That's what happened in Ephesus.

I want that in my day.

This isn't a pipe dream meant only for yesteryear. We can fight for it today. We can pray for it. We can organize ourselves and get after it. I'm driven by the reality that the kingdom of God is *now*, not later. It's here right now. It's pushing back what's dark, and it's establishing light. And you and I have been invited into it.

In the Gospels, every time Jesus performed a miracle, He was showing us what the kingdom looks like:

> When He healed the sick, He was demonstrating that the kingdom drives out sickness.
> When He raised the dead, He was demonstrating that the kingdom has victory over death.

THIS ISN'T A PIPE DREAM MEANT ONLY FOR YESTERYEAR.

When He calmed the waters, He was demonstrating that the kingdom of God is at hand.

Jesus came preaching the gospel of the kingdom, announcing that the reign of sin and death was over. It was on the clock. And now it's only a matter of time before the whole universe sees it clearly.

For you history buffs, when the beach at Normandy was taken, it was only a matter of time until the German Nazis would be defeated. Once we had that stronghold there at Omaha Beach, it was over. It was just a matter of time. Today, that's where we are. Sure, we still have a fight in front of us. Yet the beachhead has been set.

> **EVERYTHING ABOUT THIS IGNITES MY HOLY IMAGINATION.**

This idea, this possibility, provokes my spirit. It's how I'm wired. I'm here for it. Theologian Michael Bird writes, "Satan's force is spent and his worst was no match for the best of the Son of God. The fatal wound of Jesus deals a fatal blow to death. The powers of this present darkness shiver as the looming tsunami of the kingdom of God draws ever nearer. The despots of the world live in denial as much as they live on borrowed time. This is Paul's atonement theology; this is the victory of God."[1]

Everything about this ignites my holy imagination.

The first eight to ten years I was pastoring, I asked, "How? How did the Christian faith take over the world?" Because within three hundred years of the ascension of Christ, 51 percent of the Roman Empire called Christ King. Those conversions were happening while the Roman authorities were burning believers alive. While they were killing early followers of Jesus.

How did this happen? How did the darkest, most violent, sexually liberal empire the world had ever seen get overcome? And by people who didn't have political power! The Christians were marginalized. They were predominantly poor. How did it happen? How did they—and how do we—overthrow with quiet submission? This question has *gripped* me, holding me captive.

Rome couldn't figure out what was going on. Who *were* these people? The Romans didn't know. They looked at the way Christians were living, and they were baffled. They tried to kill Christians because if you're afraid of something, the best thing to do is attack it violently. And that was Rome's play. Rome was threatened because Christians changed culture.

I know we can do it today, because after Christ came on the scene, His followers did it. We can transform culture.

REFLECT

1. How would our culture be different if Christians rose up and transformed it?

   _____
   _____
   _____
   _____
   _____
   _____
   _____

2. Will you dream this big dream with me? Or does it feel *too* big? Explain your answer.

   _____
   _____
   _____
   _____
   _____
   _____
   _____

CHALLENGE

The challenge for today is another one that I hope will burrow its way into your deep places and take root inside you. The challenge is to imagine how Christians today might transform our culture so that it looks different than it does now. So that it looks more like heaven. This challenge, using Jesus' own prayer, His own words in Matthew 6:10, is, "Your kingdom come, your will be done, on earth as it is in heaven." This expansive dream wasn't too big for Jesus. Amen? So I want you to pray. I want you to cling to God's Word. And I want you to ask that the Spirit would ignite your holy imagination to begin to imagine how Christians, today, are being called to transform culture.

DAY 21
BE GENEROUS

Now the full number of those who believed were of one heart and soul, and no one said that any of the things that belonged to him was his own, but they had everything in common. And with great power the apostles were giving their testimony to the resurrection of the Lord Jesus, and great grace was upon them all. There was not a needy person among them, for as many as were owners of lands or houses sold them and brought the proceeds of what was sold and laid it at the apostles' feet, and it was distributed to each as any had need.

ACTS 4:32–35

EVERY OTHER FRIDAY, Susan cleaned the home that Mariella shared with her husband and three young kids. And while Mariella was often on her way out to the office when Susan showed up in the morning, she would pause to chat and ask Susan, who was a single mom raising four kids, about her family. One morning she learned that Susan's eldest would begin taking classes at the local city college and needed a laptop. Mariella discussed it with her husband, and they decided that the summer trip they'd planned for their family could be dialed back to be simpler and more affordable. Very quietly, Mariella gave to Susan the amount of money for the best laptop a college freshman could have. Plus a bit more. Though they mentioned it to no one, the accountant who helped them with finances was confused. He was simply baffled that the couple would practice such radical generosity.

> **THEY ARE IN LACK OF ALL THINGS, AND YET ABOUND IN ALL.**

In the first century, there were a number of practices that blew the minds of those who were living in Rome. The writings we have from that period reveal that the thinkers of the day were baffled by other mind-blowing behaviors they witnessed in the Christian community.[1] Writings from the period reveal their wonder at what they were seeing:

"They are poor, yet make many rich."

"They are in lack of all things, and yet abound in all."

In other words, they were short of everything and yet had plenty of everything. Early Christians practiced such radical generosity, which likely led to a simpler lifestyle than their contemporaries that might've seemed absurd at that moment in history.[2] Those around them simply did not know what to make of the early believers.

BE GENEROUS | 121

> They have nothing. They've chosen to live way below their means.
> Nobody does this.
> This is crazy.

(I'm paraphrasing the research, but you get the idea.)

What would that even look like today? What would that type of kindness and generosity look like on social media? What would it look like to do good, to bless those who attacked you? Because, as Jesus said in Matthew 5:11–12, if they attacked Him and all the prophets before us, it means we're probably doing something right. (One disclaimer: You might be a jerk. If you're getting pushback for being a jerk, that's not what I'm talking about. That's on you.)

> **THE FIRST-CENTURY CHRISTIANS BLEW THE MINDS OF THOSE AROUND THEM WITH THEIR GENEROSITY.**

I've got more. In his *Apology*, Aristides wrote to Roman emperor Hadrian about these new followers of Jesus and said, "They love one another. . . . And when they see a stranger, they take him in to their homes and rejoice over him as a very brother; for they do not call them brethren after the flesh, but brethren after the spirit and in God. . . . And if there is among them any that is poor and needy, and if they have no spare food, they fast two or three days in order to supply to the needy their lack of food. . . . Such is their manner of life. . . . This is a new people, and there is something divine in the midst of them."[3]

The first-century Christians blew the minds of those around them with their generosity. And that's what we were made to do too. I want to share with you a prayer we've been praying at The Village Church. It's a prayer for generosity. And the reason we repeat it often is so that it washes over us like a soaker hose. We have asked God to let this prayer form us:

> *Holy Father, there is nothing we have that You have not given us. All we have and all we are belongs to You, with the blood of Jesus. To spend selfishly and to give without sacrifice is the way of the world. But generosity is the way of those who call Christ their Lord. So help us to increase in generosity until it can be said that there is no needy person among us. Help us to be trustworthy with such a little thing as money, that You may trust us with true risks. Above all, help us to be generous because You, Father, are generous. May we show what You are like to all the world. Amen.*

Generosity is one of the primary markers that is visible in the people of God when the arrival of Light in the world caused darkness to flee. Throughout Christian history, whenever the gospel is making inroads, whenever the kingdom is being established, we see believers being crazy generous.

Let's wake up to that radical generosity.

REFLECT

1. What did you think about the gift Mariella and her husband offered to Susan? Depending on your circumstances, how easy or difficult would a comparable act of generosity—one that required sacrifice—be for you?

_____
_____
_____
_____
_____

2. When have you given generously, in a way that cost you?

_____
_____
_____
_____
_____
_____

CHALLENGE

I think you know what's coming. *Sorry, not sorry.* I want you to begin entertaining the possibility of living with radical generosity. But I'm not going to ask you to give big at this moment. Let's get your heart and wallet ready first. For today's challenge, I want you to make a choice in which you purpose to live below your means. Anyone can do this! Maybe you'll cut out your daily Frappuccino and redirect those funds—you know how much they are—to a pot that will allow you to be generous to someone else sometime soon. Or you might choose to do some kind of staycation rather than paying big bucks for a beachfront condo this summer. Ask God to guide you as you make one decision to live not just within but below your means to prepare you for radical generosity.

DAY 22: LEAVE YOUR ANXIETY WITH GOD

> "As for what was sown among thorns, this is the one who hears the word, but the cares of the world and the deceitfulness of riches choke the word, and it proves unfruitful."
>
> **MATTHEW 13:22**

JANAE HAD BEEN dreaming of owning her own catering business for years. She'd heard the stories of how hard it would be to succeed in the venture, but she had crossed every t and dotted every i. She'd done her homework. She'd secured funding. She found a storefront location. She launched with a beautiful gala.

The launch came three weeks before the COVID-19 pandemic shut down the world. Suddenly, no one was gathering in homes or even backyards to celebrate birthdays and anniversaries and graduations. Suddenly, no one needed charcuterie boards or finger sandwiches for any kind of social gathering at all.

Do you remember what was happening in your life right before it was upended by the pandemic? Back then, a lot of people had goals and plans. They were graduating from college. They were starting businesses. Getting pregnant. Planning vacations. A lot of us imagined that we were on top of things. We thought we were running our lives. And then . . . the pandemic happened.

When that happened, we weren't quietly lulled to sleep. No, it was an old-school choke out. People were being crushed by the cares of this world because we were racked with uncertainty and anxiety. We couldn't go to work, the store, or the bank. We didn't know how things would unfold, and a lot of us were scared. Concerned. Anxious. Afraid. Today, we can look back and know how it would all pan out: how we would get groceries, figure out working remotely, be in public with masks—and then there would be medicine. But as it was happening, we had no idea what would happen next.

> **IT CAN BE SO EASY TO BE DONE IN BY THE CARES OF THE WORLD.**

I'll suggest that while the COVID pandemic was unusual, it wasn't unique. No, this is how we are. We are fragile and small, and uncertainty is a certainty for us all. Uncertainty and anxiety choke us. We think we have control, and then suddenly we have no control—despite our deep desire to control things. And it slowly strangles the life out of us. And the next thing we know, we're sleeping like the early church was sleeping in Ephesus.

I don't know what this looks like in your life, but I'm curious.

What do you do when you are no longer the master of your domain? When you receive the diagnosis. When you can't make the car payment. When you get fired. When your spouse leaves. It can be so easy to be done in by the cares of the world. We're done in by anxiety. By uncertainty. We've lived it. We know it. It's thorny. When the seed the sower has sown is choked out by the cares of the world, we are put in a kind of sleeper hold that puts us to sleep.

And we also get taken out by the deceitfulness of riches. I don't mean money, because the Bible doesn't condemn making bank or having riches. The Bible warns us about the *love* of riches (1 Timothy 6:10) because that's where we get deceived. And this word isn't just for rich people. It's for folks without much money too. Any of us can be deceived into thinking, *If I just had more, my life would work.*

> OUR MONEY SEEMS TO SATISFY, SO WE'RE NO LONGER HUNGRY FOR THE THINGS OF GOD.

The cares of this world—that we can experience as the deceitfulness of riches—lull to sleep the rich and the poor. Among the rich there's a confidence in wealth that dulls our appetite for God. If we're rich, we might be trusting in money to satisfy us with the second car and the beach house and the exotic vacations. Who needs God? For the moment, our money seems to satisfy, so we're no longer hungry for the things of God.

If we don't have access to financial resources, we might naturally

128 | AWAKE AND ALIVE

believe that having money would solve everything. In both cases, we'd be wrong. We believe the lie that having more money will make everything better. (Some things? Yes. The things that matter most? No way.)

When Jesus talked about seed being scattered on thorny ground, He was talking about both the anxieties that are bullying us and also our temptation to make money our god. But the good news is that we can pivot, today. We can live as those who invest in our relationship with God, dropping every care and concern at His feet.

REFLECT

1. Whether they are urgent or whether you've got them on the back burner, what are the anxieties, worries, or concerns that you are carrying today?

___

2. Have you been fooled, in whatever way, by the deceitfulness of riches? In what ways has your relationship to money been like those thorns that choke us out?

___

CHALLENGE

The lie, or deceitfulness, of anxiety is the belief that God will not provide what we need. The lie, or deceitfulness, of riches is that we are entirely responsible for providing what we need. Both lies choke the life out of us. Today, take one action to reject these lies. If things feel tight financially, live into the reality that God is your provider by giving a gift to someone else in need. If things feel comfortable financially, do the same thing, but *go big*! Give more than what might feel safe. And remember, this isn't one of those exercises that's a magic trick where a wizard in the sky pays you back double if you have enough faith. No, this is better. This challenge strengthens your rootedness in God.

DAY 23
PLANT TREES AND LIVE FAITHFULLY

The end of all things is near. Therefore be alert and of sober mind so that you may pray. Above all, love each other deeply, because love covers over a multitude of sins. Offer hospitality to one another without grumbling. Each of you should use whatever gift you have received to serve others, as faithful stewards of God's grace in its various forms. If anyone speaks, they should do so as one who speaks the very words of God. If anyone serves, they should do so with the strength God provides, so that in all things God may be praised through Jesus Christ.

1 PETER 4:7–11 NIV

A FEW YEARS ago, I was invited to speak at a large college ministry event in College Station, Texas. The summer that Jesus really got hold of my heart in the '90s, it wasn't uncommon for me to hop in the car with a buddy and drive to this same college ministry on a Tuesday night. Back then, we met in a church sanctuary to worship and hear from the Word. Now it has grown so large it meets in the basketball arena at Texas A&M.

As I was standing in front of these students, it hit me that 90 percent of the people sitting in the arena hadn't been born yet when I was doing all that. I was blown away by how fast time is moving. The Bible paints a picture of your life and mine that is fleeting and quick. It might seem heavy, but it's true: In the expanse of an eternal God, your life is brief. So how are we meant to live in this short moment we're given?

> **HOW ARE WE MEANT TO LIVE IN THIS SHORT MOMENT WE'RE GIVEN?**

First Peter 4 cautions us away from the idea that happiness is our main goal in this short life—an idea that's as modern as it is misleading. Instead, Peter painted a picture where suffering is part of the package. It's something we all will face. Yet Jesus remains undeniably good. His words here are a call to arm ourselves with this mindset, to learn to see God's goodness no matter what.

My own seismic shift happened one Thanksgiving morning. I had a seizure that led to a grim prognosis of living just a few more years. Despite all I knew theologically, the proverbial floor fell out from under me. I wish I could tell you that in that moment I thought, *Oh,*

God's going to be glorified in huge ways. I didn't. I thought, *I want to walk my daughters down the aisle. I want to watch my son become a man. I do not want another man to marry my wife. I want to grow old with my friends. I want to be on the back porch of somebody's house as an eighty-year-old, drinking coffee and celebrating what Jesus did.* If I'm honest, I felt betrayed by the Lord.

But God pulled me back to the bigger picture. The community of faith gathered around me, caring for me, reminding me that Jesus was good even while I suffered. We need to be armed and ready because suffering will come. Peter urged us to live faithfully—not through grand gestures or big visions but by loving and serving in simple acts every day.

> **THE GREATNESS THAT JESUS IS CALLING YOU TO IS FAITHFULNESS RIGHT WHERE YOU ARE.**

There's a story that tells how someone once asked the Protestant Reformer Martin Luther what he would do if the world was ending, and he reportedly said, "If the world was to end tomorrow, I would still plant an apple tree today."[1] I don't know if he actually said that, or if I agree with all of that, but do you get the meaning behind it? The greatness that Jesus is calling you to is faithfulness right where you are.

Be faithful to your marriage; be faithful to your friends.

Be faithful to Christ in the little things at work and at home and in your community.

Be faithful where you are because Christian hope means doing whatever you've been tasked with for His glory and your joy.

He has already given you His perfection, so you don't have to struggle to earn it. Your work is faithfulness every day, right where you are.

REFLECT

1. If you're feeling overwhelmed today, pause and breathe. What's the simplest step of faithfulness you can take right now?

   _____
   _____
   _____
   _____
   _____

2. What's your attitude toward suffering? Sit with the reality that suffering is inevitable, and Jesus is good. How do these truths shift your view of faithfulness?

   _____
   _____
   _____
   _____
   _____

CHALLENGE

Reflect on life's fleeting nature today, and consider what faithfulness looks like for you. Is it reaching out to someone, serving your community, or offering kindness? Engage in small acts of faithfulness today, remembering that Christ's perfection has already been given to you.

DAY 24: BRING YOUR SIN TO GOD

"For God did not send his Son into the world to condemn the world, but in order that the world might be saved through him. Whoever believes in him is not condemned, but whoever does not believe is condemned already."

JOHN 3:17–18

EVERY DAY WE hear about people committing adultery. They step out of their marriage; they find someone on the side. And quite often these situations lead to divorce. They don't *always* lead to divorce though. Sometimes people find a way to work through adultery, to heal together. But oftentimes, adultery will end a marriage.

There is a couple at our church who was tangled up in this very mess. One had cheated on the other. And, like so many marriages, it led to divorce. But buckle your seat belt, because this couple did not *stay* divorced. And I don't mean they hurried off to marry other people. I mean that God did an amazing thing in both of their lives, and they got remarried to *each other*. Again. And on the day they shared their testimony in church, we had about fifteen people come forward to confess that they'd had an affair they'd been keeping secret. I warn you—you've got to be careful with these testimonies of what God's up to! And God was really busy in that season.

It was incredible to see those fifteen folks come forward, but all knew it was rare. Because what we do more often with our sin is the opposite of what God does with our sin. Namely, we hide it.

We stash a full bottle, hidden, in the back of our bedroom closet.

When we start sleeping with the person we're dating, we keep it from our best friend.

When we think we can cheat the government out of some tax money, we convince ourselves that if we never get audited, then our choices don't really count against us.

We convince ourselves that we can do whatever it is if we can keep it hidden.

The very last thing we want is for people to find out. The very last thing we want is for God to find out. And without even realizing it, we separate ourselves from God.

We do the opposite of what will set us free.

We were made to experience the presence of God, and it is *redemptive*. When we bring our sins to God, He can transform us. I know a lot of people who've hidden certain parts of their lives that they think won't be welcomed in the presence of God. So

> **WHEN WE BRING OUR SINS TO GOD, HE CAN TRANSFORM US.**

they give this little bit of themselves to the Lord. They've got two lives going. And that's exhausting.

The presence of God beckons us into wholeness. In John 3:17–18, Jesus welcomed us, saying, "For God did not send his Son into the world to condemn the world, but in order that the world might be saved through him. Whoever believes in him is not condemned, but whoever does not believe is condemned already." The presence of God redeems people just like you and me. This is not my opinion; it's recorded in the Bible.

In the first century, Saul of Tarsus was this dude running around killing Christians. We would *hate* him. And we would cheer if God killed him. But on the way to Damascus, Saul encountered Jesus and got redeemed (Acts 9:1–9).

What about the woman caught in adultery? Her story was redeemed by Jesus (John 8:3–11).

Throughout the Scriptures, we see those who encounter the presence of the living God being redeemed. Whatever junk we're hauling around, He takes it from us. And it's so different from how we'd play it. He invites us, *Don't hide that from Me. Get it into My presence. I'm going to do something with it that will blow your mind.*

> **WHATEVER JUNK WE'RE HAULING AROUND, HE TAKES IT FROM US.**

What about Moses? I am not playing when I say that he would not pass the background check to work at our church: "So tell us about this guy you murdered

140 | AWAKE AND ALIVE

with your bare hands. Because it seems like you've got a real rage problem, buddy."

We could do this all day.

David is called a man after God's own heart (1 Samuel 13:14; Acts 13:22). In what world? Liar. Murderer. Adulterer.

The Lord can hold things in tension that we can't.

The presence of God is redemptive.

We weren't made to read the Bible in order to learn facts about God. No, like Paul, like the woman caught in adultery, like Moses, and like David, we were made to encounter the presence of the living God. And when we do, our lives will never be the same again.

REFLECT

1. What do you think about the folks described in today's reading who came forward, publicly, to confess their sin? Have you ever had an experience like that?

_____
_____
_____
_____
_____
_____

2. How would it feel to you for others to discover the sin you wish to keep hidden from the world?

_____
_____
_____
_____
_____
_____
_____

CHALLENGE

Whatever sin you have in your life, it's just going to fester in the dark. Whatever you're trying to hide is only going to bully you and keep you captive. The way to freedom is to bring what's hidden in the dark out into the light. Today, I want you to get really honest about the sin in your life that you'd prefer to hide from others. And I want you to bring it not only to God but also to another person. Choose a friend or mentor who's spiritually grounded, and share with them the sin you'd rather hide. Pray together, offering it to God, and continue to check in with each other about what's happening in that area of your life.

DAY 25
LOOSEN YOUR GRIP

Each one must give as he has decided in his heart, not reluctantly or under compulsion, for God loves a cheerful giver. And God is able to make all grace abound to you, so that having all sufficiency in all things at all times, you may abound in every good work. As it is written, "He has distributed freely, he has given to the poor; his righteousness endures forever."

He who supplies seed to the sower and bread for food will supply and multiply your seed for sowing and increase the harvest of your righteousness. You will be enriched in every way to be generous in every way, which through us will produce thanksgiving to God.

2 CORINTHIANS 9:7–11

"**SO I WROTE** the check and gave it to the church. It was for two thousand three hundred eighty-two dollars and thirty-six cents."

If you've been around the church for a minute, you've likely heard some of these stories about what happens to people when they give to the church in faith. Do you know where this is going?

"I put it in the offering plate. And I was like, 'Lord, I don't know how we're going to do this. I just trust You.'"

Then the next day, this person goes out to the mailbox, opens it, and finds a random note from Aunt Sally. And Aunt Sally has sent them a check for $2,382.36. I know you've heard this story.

Now let me tell you *my* story.

> **DON'T GIVE UNDER COMPULSION. DON'T GIVE RELUCTANTLY.**

A number of years ago, I started making money through what the kids would call a "side hustle." (I'll just leave you to guess what it was. That's fun.) I was making some extra money, and for whatever reason, I never tithed on that. The way I saw it was that because that income wasn't showing up in my regular paycheck, it was just kind of . . . *mine*. In my mind, since I was tithing on my paycheck, the logic was sound.

I was out on one of these retreats I do with the Lord, and God rebuked me in a real kind of way about that. So I called up some of my crew and confessed it. And I wrote a check to the church to make up for my foolishness.

A few days later, I discovered that our home needed a $20,000 foundation repair.

So that happened.

That's my story. Old Aunt Sally ain't puttin' nothing in the mailbox for Matt. But here's what I got: the wrestle of faith. And that's better.

I got to say to God, "You are Lord over all time and space, and I trust You. Despite my clamoring and manipulating and maneuvering, I trust You. You're my Father; You're my King. I'm trusting You."

The word from Paul to the church in Corinth in 2 Corinthians 9:6–11 makes it plain: *Be cheerful givers*. We get our word *hilarious* from the same root as the Greek word Paul used here for "cheerful." Maybe he was saying, "Don't give reluctantly." Don't give because you know you should. Don't let somebody pull the strings on you. Don't look at Sarah McLachlan singing with a puppy and say, "Oh, take my money, because this makes me feel bad right now." Don't give under compulsion. Don't give reluctantly.

I want to be really honest about what my giving looked like early on. I started noticing that my wallet was tied to my heart in ways I didn't like. There were times when I'd give reluctantly. Or I'd feel manipulated to give. It would mess with my emotions. So the question, then, is, How do we cultivate a heart that gives cheerfully, joyfully, hilariously, without being driven by reluctance or compulsion?

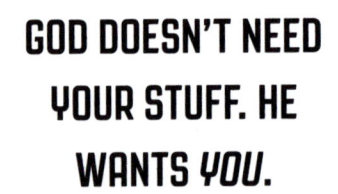

Well, the first thing is that it requires me to orient my heart rightly around God. The only way you can really be a cheerful giver is for you to know that God is generous and that everything you

> **GOD DOESN'T NEED YOUR STUFF. HE WANTS *YOU*.**

have is a gift from Him. So why wouldn't you be gracious to others? Do you see what He's doing? He's not after your wallet; He's after your heart. God doesn't need your stuff. He wants *you.*

So the lesson from Paul in 2 Corinthians 9 is that everything we have is God's, is *from* God, and is for His glory and not our self-exultation. If you see your stuff like that, if you see your free time like that, if you see your money like that, if you see your gifts like that, then that frees you up to give cheerfully.

REFLECT

1. Are you familiar with the faulty mindset that says when we give to God, we do it in a sort of manipulative way so that God is somehow obliged to bless us in return? In what ways do you tend to have that mindset?

_____
_____
_____
_____
_____
_____

2. When is a time that you have given sacrificially? When have you given and it really cost you something?

_____
_____
_____
_____
_____
_____

CHALLENGE

I hope you got warmed up in Day 21's challenge by dialing back your spending. By sacrificing a little something. By setting something aside. Because now is where it gets fun. Now you get to *give*. And I want to suggest three qualities of this giving challenge:

1. It's cheerful. It's hilarious. (If you're not there yet, ask God to help you.)
2. It's sacrificial. There's some way in which it costs you something.
3. It's private. No one on earth needs to know about it. (Unless you share finances with someone. That's the exception.)

I want you to really enjoy this challenge. Ask God to show you someone with a need today, and then enjoy your giving as the secret you share with God until the next time He invites you to do it again. And you cheerfully agree.

DAY 26
REJOICE WHEN YOU REORIENT

Rejoice in the Lord always; again I will say, rejoice. Let your reasonableness be known to everyone. The Lord is at hand; do not be anxious about anything, but in everything by prayer and supplication with thanksgiving let your requests be made known to God. And the peace of God, which surpasses all understanding, will guard your hearts and your minds in Christ Jesus.

PHILIPPIANS 4:4–7

"HEY, MOM, I can't get off the couch."

When Katie was thirty-two, she contracted Lyme disease. This young, energetic former college athlete was exhausted to the point of immobility. And the day she couldn't get up to get her two-year-old daughter upstairs after a nap, she had to call her mom for help.

That same year, Katie's dad went to be with the Lord. He was the kind of dad who was the cornerstone of the family, the kind of guy who just made everything better. The loss was sudden and disorienting.

Two years later, Katie battled endometriosis, which resulted in a hysterectomy.

Six months after the surgery, Katie wanted to get back in shape. She was doing some light lunges and felt a twinge in her hip. That twinge became an incredibly horrible pain. Now she *really* couldn't make it upstairs to cuddle with her girls.

During what should have been the most active and vibrant part of her life, Katie became a spectator as her family went swimming and skiing. When physical therapy didn't work, doctors began pain management. The dose of the pain meds was so high that she was constantly high while still in excruciating pain.

One afternoon, a number of us gathered and prayed over Katie, our tears landing on her head, and we asked that Jesus would heal her. After that prayer, the pain was gone. Zero pain. He healed her! She bounded up and down the stairs in the family's home all day long. To say we were all freaking out was an understatement.

Three days later, the pain returned.

"Hey, God, that's not nice."

> **IT'S POSSIBLE TO LIVE A LIFE OF REJOICING REGARDLESS OF YOUR CIRCUMSTANCES.**

Those were my words. But if you asked Katie, she would name those three days as a reminder of God's love for her. During those three days of relief, she heard the Lord saying, *I see you. I haven't forgotten you. And I've kept every one of your tears.*

Katie had surgery on her hip. And later that week, she had an unexplained headache and spinal issue. She lost motor function, and she couldn't walk or use her hands. A diverticulitis attack added three days to that hospital stay. A second hip surgery was a total hip replacement. As I write this, her hips are swollen in pain.

And guess what? If you saw Katie today, you'd have no idea. You'd never know that it's just been wave after wave after wave after wave of this for a decade.

I want you to know that it's possible to live a life of rejoicing regardless of your circumstances. I want you to know that in the Bible, Job wasn't some fictional character who couldn't possibly have trusted God. I want you to believe that it is possible to find goodness when all that you feel in your body is badness.

Maybe you can relate to Katie's story.

Or maybe you haven't been hit with multiple waves like she has.

Maybe for you it was just one giant tsunami that snatched your soul.

Or maybe you've lived a life full of chronic paper cuts and disappointments. You thought your life was going to be much different than it's been.

If any of these resonate with you, you're in good company. You are not alone. You are experiencing life in a fallen world. Even Jesus Himself let His disciples know, "In the world you will have tribulation. But take heart; I have overcome the world" (John 16:33).

Sometimes in Christian circles we don't want to admit that things actually hurt. So we feel like we can't pray the prayers that are in the Bible. The promise of the Bible is that God is with you in it. Jesus is with you. And He's saying, "Come to me, all you who are weary and burdened, and I will give you rest" (Matthew 11:28 NIV).

Beloved, Jesus is waiting for you to crash into His loving arms.

> **YOU CAN BRING YOUR WHOLE MESSY, DISAPPOINTED, BROKEN, ANGRY, SAD, HURTING SELF.**

You can bring your whole messy, disappointed, broken, angry, sad, hurting self. You can be honest. And, like precious Katie, with honesty, integrity, and grit, you can also rejoice in the Lord.

REFLECT

1. What do you think of Katie's steadfast confidence in God's love and goodness?

   _____
   _____
   _____
   _____
   _____
   _____
   _____

2. How difficult or easy is it for you to trust God through difficult circumstances?

   _____
   _____
   _____
   _____
   _____
   _____
   _____

CHALLENGE

Today, are you disappointed in the Lord? Do you feel like He betrayed you? You don't have to keep carrying that. One of those Scripture verses that no one's stitching on a pillow or getting inked on their arm is Jeremiah 20:7, which says, "O Lord, you have deceived me, and I was deceived." Jeremiah was saying, "God, this is rough." He continued, "I have become a laughingstock all the day; everyone mocks me." Or what about Psalm 13:1, in which David, a man after God's own heart, asked, "How long, O Lord?" *Like, really, how long? How much longer do we have to do this?* "Will you forget me forever?" No one's getting those words tattooed on their forearm. But today, these are the prayers I want you to pray. I want you to be praying honest prayers like Jeremiah and David did. God never despises an honest prayer.

DAY 27
GIVE FOR THE GOOD OF YOUR SOUL

And when Jesus came to the place, he looked up and said to him, "Zacchaeus, hurry and come down, for I must stay at your house today." So he hurried and came down and received him joyfully. And when they saw it, they all grumbled, "He has gone in to be the guest of a man who is a sinner." And Zacchaeus stood and said to the Lord, "Behold, Lord, the half of my goods I give to the poor. And if I have defrauded anyone of anything, I restore it fourfold." And Jesus said to him, "Today salvation has come to this house, since he also is a son of Abraham. For the Son of Man came to seek and to save the lost."

LUKE 19:5–10

LET'S TALK ABOUT money again. It's fun.

Okay, maybe it's not fun. But it's *necessary*. Throughout the Scriptures, in both the Old and New Testaments, the Bible makes it plain that our dollars can't be divorced from our hearts. Our monthly credit card statements are directly tied to the condition of our hearts.

When it comes to people and money, there are four types of people. I've heard it explained this way:

There are righteous rich people.
There are unrighteous rich people.
There are righteous poor people.
There are unrighteous poor people.

You get it, right? I'll bet that with no further explanation, you could identify someone who fits each of these descriptions.

This breakdown helps us avoid what some call "poverty theology." Poverty theology says that if you're a Christian, you should be poor. That's the poverty gospel. And I'll bet you already know the flip side, don't you? Because the prosperity gospel says that if you're really walking with the Lord, you'll be blessed financially.

So you've got the prosperity gospel, and that's trash. And

> **OUR SOCIOECONOMIC STATUS IS NOT AN INDICATION OF HOW GOD HAS EITHER BLESSED US OR CURSED US.**

you've got the poverty gospel, and that's also trash. Because we know that there are unrighteous wealthy people, and there are righteous poor people. Our socioeconomic status is not an indication of how God has either blessed us or cursed us. *Can I get a witness?*

We see it in Scripture. In Acts 16:14–15, Lydia from Philippi seemed to be in the fashion business, and she was killing the game. Then she encountered the gospel, and she began to see her wealth differently and to use her wealth differently for the kingdom. She was a righteous rich person.

Do you know the story of Zacchaeus? Before he met Jesus, this guy was a total schmuck: thieving, conniving, lying, manipulating to gain wealth. He was that unrighteous rich person. But when he met Jesus, when he was converted, Luke 19:1–10 shows that he began to move in the way of generosity, giving money to everyone from whom he'd stolen.

How about the unrighteous poor person? We see that in Proverbs. There are people who are poor because they're unrighteous. There are entitled sluggards who just won't work. They don't hold on to a job. They drink away or gamble away their money (Proverbs 6:6–11; 26:13–16).

The righteous poor person is the one who honors God, but the reward isn't in their Venmo account.

Here's what Jesus said about money: "Do not lay up for yourselves treasures on earth, where moth and rust destroy and where thieves break in and steal, but lay up for yourselves treasures in heaven, where neither moth nor rust destroys and where thieves do not break in and steal. For where your treasure is, there your heart will be also" (Matthew 6:19–21).

You see what He's after? Again: It's your heart.

How about Paul in Philippians 4? In verses 11–13, he said something like, "I've been poor and in prison, and I stayed at Lydia's fancy house. I can do all things through Christ. I can be really broke, or I can have cash. I can do both, and it is Christ who strengthens me either way." He went on to thank the church at Philippi for funding his ministry, and then he took a turn in verse 17 and said, basically, "But it was for you. It wasn't for me; it was for you that you gave." So Paul's argument is that you give for the good of your own soul. That tracks, right?

Do you know what's true of both the righteous person who is poor and the righteous person who is rich? They've got a loose grip. They hold what they have lightly because they know where it comes from. It's why Zacchaeus released his grip on the money he'd stolen. It's why Lydia used her resources to support kingdom work.

Loosen your hands on what God has given and walk in generosity.

> **LOOSEN YOUR HANDS ON WHAT GOD HAS GIVEN AND WALK IN GENEROSITY.**

REFLECT

1. When you consider the four categories of wealth, in which one do you find yourself? How do you feel about what you're noticing?

_____

_____

_____

_____

_____

_____

2. How easy or difficult is it for you to obey God when He instructs you to give generously? Would you say you have a loose grip and it's easy for you to give generously, or are you more naturally tightfisted?

_____

_____

_____

_____

_____

_____

CHALLENGE

Today's challenge has to do with where you located yourself in those four wealth quadrants. Specifically, ask God how He wants you to respond today based on what you've discovered:

- If you find yourself in either of the "righteous" categories, thank God for the good work He's already done in you. Then ask Him what your next righteous step should be as a giver.
- If you find yourself in either of the "unrighteous" categories, you have an opportunity to let God work through you in a way He hasn't before. Ask God to continue to guide you into paths of righteousness for the sake of your soul.

DAY 28
DELIGHT IN GOD'S PRESENCE

Then Job arose and tore his robe and shaved his head and fell on the ground and worshiped. And he said, "Naked I came from my mother's womb, and naked shall I return. The Lord gave, and the Lord has taken away; blessed be the name of the Lord."

In all this Job did not sin or charge God with wrong.

JOB 1:20–22

I WANT TO tell you the story of two guys. They're in the middle of your Bible. And that's because there are five books in the middle that are known as the wisdom literature: Job, Psalms, Proverbs, Ecclesiastes, and Song of Solomon. These books are meant to lead us into a life of virtue and wisdom.

Job was a man who had it all: beautiful wife, seven sons and three daughters, position, power, influence, and gazillions of dollars. His kids were in the house at a party when a wind struck, and they all died in an instant. Raiders came and stole his camels, his oxen, and his donkey. Job lost all his money. He lost his health. He had *nothing*. The cultural assumption among the people was that Job must be a wicked man who did something against God, and that's why all this was happening.

Here's how Job responded: "Then Job arose and tore his robe and shaved his head and fell on the ground and worshiped. And he said, 'Naked I came from my mother's womb, and naked shall I return. The Lord gave, and the Lord has taken away; blessed be the name of the Lord.' In all this Job did not sin or charge God with wrong" (Job 1:20–22). This man was covered in boils and sores, and his life had burned to the ground. Yet he found that the presence of God was enough. That's the lesson we learn from Job's life.

> **HE FOUND THAT THE PRESENCE OF GOD WAS ENOUGH.**

Then there's the book of Ecclesiastes. Solomon, the son of David, had been gifted by God with wisdom, and he also inherited the wealthiest, most powerful empire on earth at that period in human history. And he was like, "I'm gonna test it all out." So he kept his wisdom (Ecclesiastes 2:9–10), but he went hard at it. And when he wasn't getting the same rush anymore, he went *bigger*. I'm talking the party of the century. But it was different. It stopped working for him.

DELIGHT IN GOD'S PRESENCE | 163

So what he did was start building a business empire. He built vineyards and homes. He built the temple. And he built his own house. And he became a kind of business czar. And then—it stopped working.

So he was like, "Well, let me just give myself over to leisure. To comfort. Let me go live out on the ranch." It was okay for a minute, but then it stopped working for him.

Then he told us this: "So I became great and surpassed all who were before me in Jerusalem. Also my wisdom remained with me. And whatever my eyes desired I did not keep from them. I kept my heart from no pleasure, for my heart found pleasure in all my toil, and this was my reward for all my toil" (Ecclesiastes 2:9–10).

He was saying, "Pleasure is pleasure. And then it's over."

Now, originally Solomon had thought, *Surely there will be some kind of wealth, some transcendent high, some transcendent victory that will satisfy me.* But . . . nope (Ecclesiastes 1:12–2:24).

The reason Job and Solomon can help us is that you and I are stuck in the middle of those two poles. But, honestly, too often we're closer to the Solomon side than the Job side. The way we get stuck is that most of us will make a decent living and think we're almost there: *Just one more car. Just one more home. Just one more*

> **IF WE'RE NOT CAREFUL, WE'LL RUN OUR WHOLE LIVES ON THAT TREADMILL AND NEVER ACTUALLY GET TO LIVE.**

zero on my income statement. Then I'll have arrived. We're test-driving the Solomon way, and if we're not careful, we'll run our whole lives on that treadmill and never actually get to live.

I want you to understand that the answer, regardless of whether your life is going well or not, is the presence of God. According to the way you were designed, the fuel of your life is meant to be the presence of God.

That's what Job was filled with.

It's what Solomon hungered for.

The story of the Bible is about the presence of God. God is not only with us, but as we go, we take Him with us in that we become the temple of the living God, the tabernacle of the holy God (1 Corinthians 6:19–20). Revelation 21:3–4 announces, "And I heard a loud voice from the throne saying, 'Behold, the dwelling place of God is with man. He will dwell with them, and they will be his people, and God himself will be with them as their God. He will wipe away every tear from their eyes, and death shall be no more, neither shall be there be mourning, nor crying, nor pain anymore, for the former things have passed away.'"

You were created to experience the presence of God, now and forevermore.

REFLECT

1. Are there ways in which you recognize yourself, or your experience, in Solomon's wild ride? In what ways have you been tempted to find satisfaction outside of God?

___

___

___

___

___

___

2. Is there a way in which you relate to Job's experience? In what ways have you been able to experience the sufficiency of God's presence, even when times have been hard?

___

___

___

___

___

___

CHALLENGE

The late pastor Tim Keller prepared a list of nine questions for sleepy Christians. (Heads up, friend. That's not someone else. It's you. He's talking to you.) And I love these questions because, on this journey into being awake and alive, they help us get a pulse on how sleepy we are. And on how deep or shallow our roots are today. Keller has nine questions, but I'm going to offer you just the first two to sit with today.[1]

1. How real has God been this week to your heart?
2. How clear and vivid is your assurance and certainty of God's forgiveness and fatherly love?

These questions are a great spiritual MRI to check the condition of your heart. Let the results guide you as you seek to enjoy God's presence.

DAY 29 CHOOSE WHAT MATTERS MOST

I bless the Lord who gives me counsel; in the night also my heart instructs me. I have set the Lord always before me; because he is at my right hand, I shall not be shaken. Therefore my heart is glad, and my whole being rejoices; my flesh also dwells secure. For you will not abandon my soul to Sheol, or let your holy one see corruption. You make known to me the path of life; in your presence there is fullness of joy; at your right hand are pleasures forevermore.

PSALM 16:7–11

WE'LL START TODAY by dropping some wisdom from some of the world's brightest minds.

There's a quote attributed to the great comedian and theologian Jim Carrey, who is rumored to have said, "I think everybody should get rich and famous and do everything they ever dreamed of." He continued, "So they can see that's not the answer."[1]

Noted.

Madonna said, "My drive in life is from this horrible fear of being mediocre. And that's always pushing me, pushing me. Because even though I've become Somebody, I still have to prove that I'm *Somebody*. My struggle has never ended and it probably never will."[2]

Heartbreaking.

How about the GOAT, Tom Brady? Years ago, he said, "Why do I have three Super Bowl rings and still think there's something greater out there for me? I mean, maybe a lot of people would say, 'Hey, man, this is what it is.' I reached my goal, my dream, my life. . . . I think, God, it's got to be more than this."[3]

Today he has seven Super Bowl rings. And he's right: There *is* more than this.

> **HE'S RIGHT: THERE *IS* MORE THAN THIS.**

On and on and on, striving after the wind. You're going to be hard-pressed to find someone really, *really* successful who can honestly report that money, fame, or power is deeply satisfying. And you know from yesterday's reading that Solomon, King David's wise son, discovered that centuries before Jim, Madonna, or Tom. He began the book of Ecclesiastes like this: "'Meaningless! Meaningless!' says the Teacher. 'Utterly meaningless! Everything is meaningless'" (1:2 NIV).

But his counterpart, Job, discovered that if you lose everything beyond your wildest imagination, if you suffer beyond your wildest imagination, you'll find that the presence of God is enough. If you get everything your heart ever desired and more, if you get that

> **IF YOU GET EVERYTHING YOUR HEART EVER DESIRED AND MORE ... IT CANNOT COMPARE TO DELIGHTING IN THE PRESENCE OF GOD.**

Bezos kind of money, it cannot compare to delighting in the presence of God. The billions of dollars? Meaningless.

This wisdom that is woven throughout the pages of the Bible is entirely counterintuitive, right? It rejects the world's values in favor of God's values. And if we're going to receive it in our deep places, we need to be very intentional about it.

So today I want to offer you a practice. You'll have the opportunity to do it yourself when we get to the challenge. I'm suggesting that we do something with our bodies because we are embodied creatures. It's why the Bible is always trying to get our bodies involved in the worship of God.

Lift your hands.
Bow down.
Clap your hands.

Here's what I'd love for you to do. I want you to get settled and take a deep breath. Then I want you to cup your hands and put them right in front of you. If it's too weird, get over it. You got this. We're going to be asking God to fill your tank, to fill you with His love. So we're positioning our bodies in a receptive posture.

I don't know how you came into today's reading. You might be filled up. Perhaps you've been walking in a rich, deep, intimate relationship with Jesus. If this is you, ask for more. He's got inexhaustible wealth. How cool is that?

But maybe you haven't been feeling God's love for you. Perhaps the idea of intimate nearness and friendship with God is something you just haven't had a category for until now. If so, I simply want you to ask, in prayer, that you might experience the love of God. (If you need to pray a "This is weird, I don't like it" prayer, you can do that. But then add, "If You're there, will You please fill my heart?")

The testimony of those who've earned all the awards and accolades and attention the world has to offer is that all of it, in the end, comes to nothing. It doesn't satisfy. It's meaningless. But the testimony of those who've made a different choice, who've opened their hearts to receive the boundless riches of God's love, tells a different story. Make it your own.

REFLECT

1. What do you make of some of the world's most successful people discovering that all the striving after success, wealth, and fame is meaningless?

_____
_____
_____
_____
_____
_____

2. And how about you today? Are you coming to God with a full cup or an empty well?

_____
_____
_____
_____
_____
_____

CHALLENGE

You already know what today's challenge is. Get comfortable, cup your hands, and take a deep breath. Your open hands are an expression of your heart's posture before God. I'll suggest a prayer you can pray.

Holy Spirit, we ask You to show us the beauty of Jesus. Will You help us experience Your love in what the apostle Paul called in 2 Corinthians 4:16 "our inner self"? We're not looking for new stuff. We want to experience Your love in the deep places of our hearts. And there's a lot fighting against that in our lives and in the world. So I ask that You would overcome those forces supernaturally and powerfully. Thank You for Your Word, for the truth of it, for the weight of it, and thank You that You minister to us deeply. Amen.

DAY 30
RESPOND TO GOD'S INVITATION

"Come, everyone who thirsts, come to the waters; and he who has no money, come, buy and eat! Come, buy wine and milk without money and without price. Why do you spend your money for that which is not bread, and your labor for that which does not satisfy? Listen diligently to me, and eat what is good, and delight yourselves in rich food. Incline your ear, and come to me; hear, that your soul may live; and I will make with you an everlasting covenant, my steadfast, sure love for David."

ISAIAH 55:1–3

WHEN IT COMES to hospitality, are you more often the inviter or the invitee?

Are you blasting your favorite tunes while you cook dinner for the neighbors down the street who will sit at your table for hours? Or—and I realize that you may experience real culinary challenges—are you more likely to be the invited guest? Do you have a friend, relative, or colleague who loves to be hospitable and have you over to dine?

When we look at the Gospels, we see exactly what kind of host Jesus is. We witness Him surprising more than five thousand friends and strangers with a satisfying meal (Matthew 14:13–21). We hear Him announcing, "I am the bread of life" (John 6:35). And when He met Zacchaeus, He announced, "I must stay at your house today" (Luke 19:5). That's Jesus-style hospitality, right there. I'm coming to your place, and I've got it covered.

We discover the invitational nature of God in Isaiah 55. God, speaking through the prophet Isaiah, said, "Come, everyone who thirsts, come to the waters; and he who has no money, come, buy and eat! Come, buy wine and milk without money and without price" (v. 1). Then came the question: "Why do you spend your money for that which is not bread, and your labor for that which does not satisfy?" (v. 2).

Next, God threw out the invitation to be in His presence: "Listen diligently to me, and eat what is good, and delight yourselves in rich food" (v. 2). He continued, "Incline

> **GOD'S PRESENCE IS INVITATIONAL. AND HE INVITES US TO LIVE *AWAKE* AND *ALIVE*.**

RESPOND TO GOD'S INVITATION | 175

your ear, and come to me; hear, that your soul may live; and I will make with you an everlasting covenant, my steadfast, sure love for David" (v. 3).

Let's stop right there. God was talking about the covenant He made with David (2 Samuel 7:8–16). He was saying to the people through Isaiah—and He's still saying to us today—"I love David, and I can love you. Have you been a murdering adulterer? Because I love David. I can love you." It's invitational. We are invited to bring our whole battered, messy selves. In Matthew 11:28, Jesus says to you and me, in essence, "Yeah, get in here. Bring the hope and the fear and the anxiety and the peace. Get it all in here. I want all of it. I want to be with you."

God's presence is invitational. And He invites us to live *awake* and *alive.*

Have you been eating animal crackers and calling it a feast? How much longer are you going to do this to yourself? Listen, there's a feast for you. In this invitation, God is talking about you.

You.

And you don't have to be able to wax eloquent, to talk fancy about doctrine and theology. A lot of people can do that and don't know anything about the presence of God or have an intimate relationship with Jesus.

Here's my question: Are you living a life of ferocious devotion? Are you experiencing everything that Jesus says life in Him ought to look like? It's the story of the Bible that you were created to know joy in His presence.

You've spent thirty days wrestling with this, searching the Scriptures, and doing the challenges. Don't stop now. Ask the Holy

Spirit to search your heart. Ask, "Where can I grow? What do I need to know? How can I experience this relationship with You? What comes next when I close this book?"

> **BELOVED, IT'S WHAT YOU WERE MADE FOR.**

Do you have an intimate relationship with God through Jesus? That is what Christianity is. That's exactly what it means to live fully awake and alive.

Beloved, it's what you were made for.

REFLECT

1. When it comes to hospitality, are you more likely to be the host who invites or the guest who accepts an invitation? Why do you think that is?

   _____
   _____
   _____
   _____
   _____
   _____

2. What comes next for you now that you've finished this challenge? What practices or habits will you make part of your ongoing desire to grow in intimacy with Jesus?

   _____
   _____
   _____
   _____
   _____
   _____

CHALLENGE

As we're wrapping this thirty-day challenge, remember that intimacy with God is not just attending a Sunday church service or reading a good book. It's a way of living your whole *life*. Continue to spend intentional time with Him daily. Come alive by connecting with Jesus in prayer, in the Bible, in service, and in giving to friends. As the Nike slogan says, today I'm encouraging you to Just Do It. That means you carve out time. You keep making it a priority. You put it on your calendar. On *repeat*.

The spiritual fathers and mothers you see who have intimacy with Jesus? It's not because they're better than you. It's because they make Him a priority, season after season. Commit to this pursuit long after you close this book. Make a plan for how you'll continue to chase after Him. I encourage you to share what's stirred in your heart throughout this journey with a mentor or friend who knows Him, and invite them to check back in with you about your commitment to prioritize Him.

You were created to live fully awake and alive. That life is found in Jesus.

You got this. Keep going.

NOTES

DAY 2: KNOW EXTERNAL TRUTH
1. *A Few Good Men*, written by Aaron Sorkin, directed by Rob Reiner (Columbia Pictures, 1992).

DAY 4: SINK DEEP ROOTS
1. Tyler Staton, *Praying Like Monks, Living Like Fools: An Invitation to the Wonder and Mystery of Prayer* (Thomas Nelson, 2022).
2. C. S. Lewis, *Letters of C. S. Lewis*, ed. W. H. Lewis (Harcourt Brace, 1993), 395.

DAY 9: GET RE-GOSPELED
1. Mark Shea, "Who Was the New Testament Written For?" The Catholic Weekly, July 11, 2021, https://catholicweekly.com.au/mark-shea-who-was-the-new-testament-written-for/.

DAY 11: RECEIVE NEW MERCIES
1. C. S. Lewis, *The Problem of Pain* (HarperOne, 2009), 96.

DAY 15: BELIEVE IN THE MIRACULOUS
1. Peter Manseau, "Why Thomas Jefferson Created His Own Bible," *Smithsonian* magazine, September 8, 2020, https://www.smithsonianmag.com/smithsonian-institution/why-thomas-jefferson-created-his-own-bible-180975716/.
2. Thomas Jefferson, *The Life and Morals of Jesus of Nazareth* (1895).

DAY 16: MATURE BY SERVING
1. The Pareto Principle, created by economist Vilfredo Pareto in the nineteenth century. In the early 1940s, Dr. Joseph Juran rediscovered Pareto's work and popularized it. "Pareto Principle (80/20 Rule) & Pareto Analysis Guide," *Juran* (blog), March 12, 2019, https://www.juran.com/blog/a-guide-to-the-pareto-principle-80-20-rule-pareto-analysis/.

DAY 20: TRANSFORM CULTURE
1. Michael F. Bird, *Evangelical Theology: A Biblical and Systematic Introduction* (Zondervan, 2013), 394–95.

DAY 21: BE GENEROUS
1. Alexander Roberts and James Donaldson, trans., "The Epistle of Mathetes to Diognetus," in *The Apostolic Fathers with Justin Martyr and Irenaeus*, Ante-Nicene Fathers, vol. 1. (Christian Literature Publishing, 1885). Revised and edited for New Advent by Kevin Knight, https://www.newadvent.org/fathers/0101.htm.
2. Peter Kirby, "Diognetus," Early Christian Writings.com, accessed March 12, 2025, https://www.earlychristianwritings.com/text/diognetus-roberts.html.
3. D. M. Kay, trans., "The Apology of Aristides," in *The Gospel of Peter [...] and Commentary on Matthew, Books 1, 2, and 10-14*, ed. Allan

Menzies (Christian Literature Publishing, 1896). Revised and edited for New Advent by Kevin Knight, https://www.newadvent.org/fathers/1012.htm.

DAY 23: PLANT TREES AND LIVE FAITHFULLY

1. Trevor Sutton, "Let It Be Done," The Lutheran Witness, November 12, 2020, https://witness.lcms.org/2020/let-it-be-done/.

DAY 28: DELIGHT IN GOD'S PRESENCE

1. Tim Keller, "Center Church: Questions for Sleepy and Nominal Christians," sermon, posted February 28, 2013, by Redeemer City to City, YouTube, https://www.youtube.com/watch?v=YsStN5kKfX4&t=1s.

DAY 29: CHOOSE WHAT MATTERS MOST

1. Jim Carrey, attributed. Jay Stone, "Carrey's Been Busted," *The Ottawa Citizen*, December 16, 2005, Newspapers.com.
2. Lynn Hirschberg, "The Misfit," *Vanity Fair*, April 1991, https://archive.vanityfair.com/article/1991/4/the-misfit.
3. Tom Brady, "Tom Brady on Winning: There's 'Got to Be More Than This,'" (interview by Steve Kroft, June 2005), posted January 30, 2019, by *60 Minutes*, YouTube, https://www.youtube.com/watch?v=-TA4_fVkv3c.

[EXCERPT]

1. "James J. Braddock," Estate of James J. Braddock, accessed November 8, 2023, https://www.jamesjbraddock.com.

ACKNOWLEDGMENTS

TO THE TEAM at HarperCollins that helped bring this project to life!

Thank you to Curtis and Karen Yates for seeing more in me than I could see in myself. What a gift your friendship and partnership these past few years have been.

Nothing really works in my life without you, Andrea Bowman. You manage my calendar, travel, and space for me to write, prepare, and preach like a boss!

Thank you, TVC, for allowing me the time and space to work outside of our family of faith. Everything I've done has been born of my time and depth with you.

To Lauren, whose voice is woven through almost everything I have ever preached and written. Where would I be without your steadfast, fierce devotion to Jesus and our family? Love you!

ABOUT THE AUTHOR

MATT CHANDLER is a husband, father, pastor, elder, and author whose greatest desire is to make much of Jesus. He has served over twenty years as the lead pastor at The Village Church in Flower Mound, Texas, which recently transitioned its five campuses into their own autonomous churches. He is also the executive chairman of the Acts 29 Network, a large church-planting community that trains and equips church planters across the globe. Matt is known worldwide for proclaiming the gospel in a powerful and down-to-earth way and enjoys traveling to share the message of Jesus whenever he can. He lives in Texas with his beautiful wife, Lauren, and their three children, Audrey, Reid, and Norah.

ALSO BY MATT CHANDLER

The Overcomers:
God's Vision for You to Thrive in an Age of Anxiety and Outrage
(See excerpt beginning on page 189.)

Enjoy this excerpt from
THE OVERCOMERS

INTRODUCTION

GOD'S SURPRISING PLAN TO PUSH BACK DARKNESS

What if I told you that you are made for this exact moment in human history? That it's not just blue check mark, celebrity Christians we need at this moment, but *you*. Not the future version of you or the person you hope to become, but *you now*! Would you roll your eyes and think, *Yeah, yeah, Pastor Matt. Sure I am.*

Or would you believe me?

What if I told you that you can be braver than you think? That you can be more confident and that you're dangerous when it comes to the enemy's work in our day? Could I convince you that you're uniquely wired and placed in this moment in human history as part of God's big plan to push back the darkness and establish light?

Not me, Matt. I'm no Mother Teresa.

You don't know my story, Matt. I'm actually a mess.

You're a pastor. You have to say that.

Yada yada . . .

What if I told you that you don't need to be anxious or afraid of anything? Would you trust me if I told you that you're not a victim and don't have to be a passive bystander?

I realize this might be hard to believe, but you're a crucial part of what God is working out in our day.

YOU ARE AN OVERCOMER

I wish we were sitting together talking over a cup of coffee at Marty B's Coffee down the road from me. I'd love to hear how God has been at work in your life and how He's led you to this book. Over a strong, long black, I'd ask you what you were hoping for when you picked it up and began reading. We'd talk about the curiosities, the stories, the doubts, and the lies you're dealing with at this very moment. Knowing these things about you would lead me to press harder on certain parts of this book and not as hard on others. There would be moments we would take a break or veer into a tangent. Or maybe we'd stop and pray or cry or laugh. Unfortunately, I don't have the luxury of sitting in person and conversing with you. It really is my preferred pastime to sit with other believers and share our stories.

And so, I write today as best I can as one who knows the Bible, as a fellow sojourner in this Christian life, and as a pastor who has witnessed the masterful ways our enemy deceives and lies to us, hoping we shrink back from the dynamic, empowered life God intends for us—the life we want for ourselves.

Despite what you and I may see, God is at work in the mess of our world and our everyday lives. Believe it or not, God is accomplishing His purposes: He is seeking and saving the lost. He is exacting justice on His creation. He is working miracles among the sick and brokenhearted. He is pouring out His grace and forgiveness on all of us.

At this very moment, God is calling people into a deeper relationship with Him—one that is built on the power and authority of Jesus. And here's the crazy part: you have been called right into the center of this ultimate reality.

Do you realize you belong to a global people who have thrived through worldwide pandemics, peacefully overthrown tyrannical empires, increased the safety and dignity of women and children around the world, and ushered in the end of a global slave trade? What if I told you that many of our nation's hospitals and orphanages have denominational names because your spiritual family cared for the sick and looked after the widows and orphans in their distress?

Your spiritual family pushed back the darkness and established order and light, even as they fought to overcome their own sins and doubts for two thousand years. It's your turn now, and you have it in you. Here is a definition of an Overcomer I've pulled from the Scriptures:

> An Overcomer is a believer propelled by scriptural truths, empowered by the work of Jesus, and encouraged by those who have gone before them. With open eyes to deeper spiritual realities, the one who overcomes endures the brokenness of the world with holy resolve. This individual, marked by love and through the power of the Holy Spirit, joins in God's offensive against darkness and destruction. The Overcomer unites with the triune God and His holy church to stand as an unwavering, unanxious presence. Bluntly put, the Overcomer is a major problem to the enemy.

During the past two thousand years, there have been extremely difficult times when our spiritual family could have wilted, fled for the hills, or silently ignored the world's pains. But God, knowing it's scary to be us, let us in on a picture of ultimate reality in the book of Revelation. That picture has put steel in the spines of our brothers and sisters across time and space, and it does the same for us today. So as you flip through the pages of this book, I want to show you this picture of ultimate reality, your place in God's divine purposes, and why Satan is terrified that you have this book in your hands.

In 1933, James J. Braddock was a has-been boxer who had lost a heavyweight title fight and never fully recovered. Had we met him that year, we would think almost everything about him was unimpressive. He was working as a longshoreman with an impaired right hand and a face that looked like he'd been smacked with a frying pan. He was trying to survive the Great Depression by working on the docks and was not really succeeding. Braddock was forced to go on government relief in an attempt to support his family.

In 1934, Braddock was given a fight against a promising and highly touted fighter named John "Corn" Griffin, whom he knocked out in the third round. After several other wins, it became apparent that not only had Braddock's right hand healed, but his left was now stronger from his work on the docks. On June 13, 1935, in the Madison Square Garden Bowl, Braddock, a ten-to-one underdog, fought the younger, stronger, and faster heavyweight champion of the world, Max Baer, and won. In what was called one of the "greatest fistic upsets" of his time, James J. Braddock, nicknamed "Cinderella Man," revealed he was stronger than people thought and had more untapped potential than anyone could have imagined.[1]

Throughout the history of the church, we have too many Cinderella men and women to count. We can easily rattle off the famous ones: the apostle John, Peter, Paul, Mary Magdalene, John the Baptist, Augustine, Martin Luther, Corrie ten Boom, John Wycliffe, John Calvin, John Wesley, C. S. Lewis, Dietrich Bonhoeffer, Florence Nightingale, Billy Graham.

But there are exponentially more obscure, remarkable, honorable, godly Christian leaders you haven't heard of. Millions, actually. Maybe you know a believer in your life, past or present, who has significantly influenced you. All these Christians were uniquely made and placed for their time for a specific God-orchestrated reason.

PAUL, I'VE HEARD OF

There's a fascinating story in Acts 19 about a group of itinerant Jewish exorcists (who knew that was a thing?) who started using the name of Jesus in an attempt to cast out demons after watching the apostle Paul do all sorts of miracles. Starting in verse 11, the passage reads:

> And God was doing extraordinary miracles by the hands of Paul, so that even handkerchiefs or aprons that had touched his skin were carried away to the sick, and their diseases left them and the evil spirits came out of them. Then some of the itinerant Jewish exorcists undertook to invoke the name of the Lord Jesus over those who had evil spirits, saying, "I adjure you by the Jesus whom Paul proclaims." Seven sons of a Jewish high priest named Sceva were doing this. But the evil spirit answered them, "Jesus I know, and Paul I recognize, but who are you?" (vv. 11–15)

Did you catch that? "Jesus I know, and *Paul I recognize*." I love that passage. Paul was wreaking so much havoc in Satan's kingdom that the demons basically said, "We've heard of him." Can you picture word spreading about Paul throughout the domain of darkness as the demons told one another about this punk guy who had been causing them all kinds of problems?

If I may put all my cards on the table here at the very beginning, this is what I'm calling you to boldly step into—to become a problem for the enemy! In the spaces you live, work, and play, you, too, can be a dynamic disrupter of the powers of this present darkness—so much that the demons recognize you (as they did Paul) as a threat to their evil plans and schemes.

More than likely, at this moment, you want to interrupt me and explain that you're no apostle Paul. Here's the thing: I know you're not. Neither am I. You're you, and I'm me. That's important because these are *our* days, not Paul's. He had his days; these are ours. God's big plan for today is *you*. Not Paul or Peter or Augustine or Charles Spurgeon or Billy Graham. You!

To understand the fullness of who we are and what our purpose is, you and I need to consider ourselves in three ways:

1. We are made in the image of God.
2. We are children of God.
3. We are uniquely wired and uniquely placed by God.

It's vital to understand we are all three of these things before we are able to step into our design and destiny and embrace what we were fully intended to be.